My Scarlet Letter

My Scarlet Letter

My Scarlet Letter
(all text, poetry, artwork)
© 2010
By Jen Dubis
All Rights Reserved
ISBN 978-0-578-06643-1

Cover Image
Original Art
© 2010
By Jen Dubis

My Scarlet Letter

Prologue
A Message from the Author
Dedications

Chapters

1 Absolute

2 Analytical

3 Anomaly

4 Anachronism

5 Anorexic

6 Agony

7 Annihilation

8 Altruistic

Epilogue

'

My Scarlet Letter

Prologue

The excruciating heat of summer absorbed into the seats of my Honda (an unpleasant downfall of leather). But it was not the burning pain from any light touch that bothered me. I had grown to tolerate and even enjoy it a bit. Sick, right? But I had just gotten into my car when that familiar sensation hit and then subsided quickly as I began to drive. But a completely different sensation shifted into gear as I stopped at a light by the railroad tracks. It felt like a mosquito was in the left arm of my sweatshirt, which annoyed me without end. I shook my arm and was convinced I had now moved it to a new home on my back which was not any easier to ignore. Yet, my arm was still itchy. So were there two mosquitoes plotting against me? I now moved to rolling up my sleeve to see if I was bitten. No bite, but my arm sure was pinker than normal.

I could not see my back, obviously, but I looked on my stomach and saw more pink blotches. I turned my focus from mosquitoes to an irritation from the fabric that was touching me. But I had worn this sweatshirt for months without issue. I should mention, however, that I had a thermal long sleeve top and a t-shirt on underneath the sweatshirt. Yes, I know it was the summer, but my Reynaud's Disease makes me more susceptible to cold and layers

My Scarlet Letter

worked for me. Again, with the top, I had worn it before with no problems.

Next step, where did I just come from? I was at a family therapy appointment sitting on a couch. Maybe there was something on the couch that somehow irritated my skin. But, wait, I had sat there before, too. Well, I strolled through the garden center at Home Depot after leaving a painting job at a client's house. Still, nothing jumped out as the culprit. I was, however, feeling heat on my body in addition to the annoying itch. For a girl who was not bothered by searing heat of the leather seats, this alarmed me but I continued on my way home.

Once there, I went into the bathroom to check out more of my skin to see if it had gone down at all. Not only did it not go away, but the blotches were now on the sides of my trunk, my belly and my arms. I put some anti-itch cream on every affected area I could see and decided to give it some time to calm down. How much time do I wait? I could not keep my mind focused on anything else but this bizarre occurrence. So an hour goes by with no improvement, but I shrug it off. The second hour I start to get a bit anxious and decide to ask my mother for her opinion. She is taken aback when I lift my shirt to show her my back and says, "It looks like hives."

"But I have never had hives before," was my response.

"Where were you today? What did you touch or eat?" asked my mother.

My Scarlet Letter

" I went to Joe's to paint my mural and then stopped at Home Depot before picking up Brian and Kristen to meet you at the therapist."
"Well, did you eat anything out of the ordinary today?" was her next inquiry.
"No, not really. So how do I fix these things?" was all I cared about at the moment.
She looked online and we tried the different remedies for a while. I had just about built up a tolerance for the heat and itching and was now in my pajamas ready to call it a night. Oddly enough, I was starting to get chilly even though my skin was on fire but I assumed it was the Reynaud's talking to me. I ended up with a blanket on me trying to shake the chill in my bones.

    Suddenly, my breath felt slower and more labored than before, but I did not say anything about it. Instead, I curled up more into my blanket. I shook my head to try and shake it off but, to my surprise, I started to shake all over. My arms and legs were flapping, as I was sitting crisscrossed on the couch. All I can say is it was so strange to not be able to control the movements. I stuck my arm out of the blanket and held it up in front of me as it shook up and down. Thinking I was exaggerating, my mother, on the opposite end of the couch, said, "Wow, you really are cold, huh?"
"Mom, I'm not doing that. It won't stop." I told her as my voice cracked a bit. "I cannot s-s-stop shaking." Immediately, she popped up from her seat and pulled the blanket off and saw my knees knocking back and forth. She attempted to

My Scarlet Letter

help me stand, but I could put no pressure on my legs. I must have been a sight to see because she also noticed blotches on my neck.

"Jen, you need to get checked out, now!" she declared with a look of fear in her eyes.

"No, no, no" was my immediate reaction to that statement. "It's nothing, I will be fine."

"Jen, this is not normal!" she urged.

"I don't want to go to the emergency room. I will not go there."

I truly did not want to be poked and prodded at the hospital looking like I did. I also knew that any doctor would certainly comment on my general health, aside from the hives and shaking. What do I mean? Well, my shoulder blades were sticking out further than most people's do and I had lost some weight. Normally, losing weight is great but I had gone beyond what everyone thought was a healthy weight. So I feared that a doctor would say that I was a hazard to myself and order me to stay there. This was the absolute last thing I wanted to hear, let alone be forced to do. But the shaking and shortness of breath did not stop and I got scared that my body was ready to shut down. Luckily, the hospital is only a few minutes from my house. In the emergency room, there were about seven other people waiting for treatment. One elderly woman I remember seeing was sitting in a wheelchair with her leg up and a dressing around her foot. There was blood soaked through the bandage and I remember feeling guilty that I was taken

My Scarlet Letter

in before she was. In my case, there were concerned of anaphylaxis and needed to control my supposed allergic reaction before my breathing was compromised. Still, I know that woman was waiting longer than I was and felt she should be seen.

    Once inside the curtain, my vitals were taken and the nurse could see the hives invading my body. At this point, they were so widespread over my body that I even had some on my scalp and in the webs of my fingers and toes. Just as one spot would calm down intensity, another spot would spike. The hours were agonizing and I was given two nebulizer treatments. The areas of my body that were not swollen and red became white and numb, thanks to Reynaud's. Hospitals are not exactly perfect in terms of temperature control but just think about being so hot on eighty percent of your body and then contrasting that with the cold, numb tingling of the extremities. I was a complete mess and petrified of having to stay there overnight. My mother knew it and could see my turmoil. Both doctors I saw told me that I may need to carry an epi-pen with me in case I should have another episode. Fortunately, my breathing improved enough after the nebulizer treatments for my to be written a prescription for Benadryl and a steroid. My mother's jaw dropped when they finally discharged me without much said about my weight. I was surprised, but very relieved. Surely they noticed, but I guess they did not care.

My Scarlet Letter

This was my experience with people's interactions with me. Something was very wrong with me, but no one knew what to do. I was an adult. I was a teacher with a Master's Degree. No one addressed it, least of all my friends. Or, maybe, they did not feel it was that serious. My mother knew before I did because I was not thinking clearly about what was happening. I just wanted to keep to myself and not bother anyone. But soon enough, my appearance bothered everyone and I could see it in the glances I received. I did not admit then, but I was rolling slowly down a very steep hill as the sky darkened and the air thickened. And in one year's time, I would be staring death in the face...not flinching at all.

My Scarlet Letter

Message from the author:

"To the finder of these writings:
Please know that I did not do this on purpose. I wanted what you want... happiness, love, health.... Never did I want to be a tragedy or a statistic. In fact, I am not a person that likes attention. I don't want people looking at me all the time, but they do now. Somehow this disease has penetrated my soul. For years, I built such a monolithic wall to protect my emotional well-being. Come to find out, it was not such a positive thing to do. It caused me to be stuck and prevented me from moving forward in life. And in order to heal, I had to break it down. Now, I could not just take a sledgehammer to the wall, rather I slowly started scratching away at it so that such a tool could do more than simply crack the foundation. This breach allowed poison to invade. You know any healing process involves pain, but I had no idea that this was the amount of paint I was destined to feel. Physically, emotionally and spiritually, the pain drains me. I wish I did not put a hole in the wall. Maybe I would have been better off. Perhaps I would not have gotten this disease. I try to do what is right and try to deal with problems on my own. I do not want it to affect others. Yes, I am of that perfectionist personality

My Scarlet Letter

type and harbor much guilt for those around me. I also over-analyze. (As my mother says, "Nothing is off my radar screen."

But I always want to figure it out and find the path to success that I can claim as my own. If I don't, I am a failure. And, boy, how I have failed at such a crucial topic- living. How hard can it be, right? Well, come to find out, I have not been living, only merely existing. I have breath in my lungs, but for how much longer? I know what you are thinking: Ok, so you are aware of all of this, so just eat and all is saved. But you do not realize that it is deeper than that. It is not a disease that is so superficial that eating food is the answer. On the surface, yes, I can see how that must seem like the answer to my health. I keep hearing a song on the radio called "Skin & Bones" and thinking about myself. I let myself get to an extremely fragile state and I never truly felt cleansed of any negativity. All I experience is hyper-vigilant awareness of my vulnerability. Why is that? I cannot ask any more questions because I don't know- I have no fucking clue why this is the story of what became of me. You hear that hope guides you and being saved is not a far-fetched fantasy. Truth be told, I hurt a lot of people because of this. My family loves me because I am family, but they hate what came with me. Without the blood connection, how could you love someone who tortures and annoys you just by looking at them? It must have been so difficult for them-to try and see the real me every single time I crossed their paths. I cannot imagine having to live in a house with

My Scarlet Letter

that after already walking on eggshells for years prior. I guess in some way, they needed to know I was still there in order to keep their own heads and hearts in the right place. Yet I was so out-of-synch and out of character. I allowed myself to believe that I was poison. I was hurting everyone and the devil that plagued me concocted plans and carried out schemes that he knew would get to me. I was the true embodiment of my own worst enemy. I never let myself acknowledge that we are works in progress and if I could not love myself one hundred percent then who the hell would want my baggage on top of theirs. Check it and chuck it. Find comfort, find support and find life. I just never knew how to use my support system in a beneficial way. I didn't quite figure it out. I should have though. I thought I was more intelligent than this. Essentially I have wasted a gift. Life was mine for the living. So many want to live and experience and do and be (myself included). Yet it was overshadowed and never a priority. Poisoned blood runs thick. It outsmarted me and took me for all I had...slowly....painfully.....without compassion or mercy."

"All I can picture as I write this is my family cleaning out my room and going through all of my stuff. The "what-stays-what-goes" phase leads to my journals and random thoughts I scribbled in private will now be in the open. It may anger and probably disappoint whoever reads the chaotic mess, this release of built-up tension and pain. My headaches need to stop. Anxiety needs to stop. Clenching

My Scarlet Letter

needs to stop. Embracing life needs to take a front seat. Right now, though, I feel as though I am embracing dirt sooner than anything else."

What you hold in your hand is not a novel in the traditional sense of the word. There are no characters or plot schemes... no beginning or end. It is not simply excerpts from a journal. No day-after-day or play-by-play of events. I'm not sure how to describe it, but I feel it is a snapshot of my struggle in hopes to help others and bring awareness to those who feel the topic is taboo. These cluttered thoughts offer no solution or steps because each person will suffer in different ways and I know that no book helped me. I found no answers and could not relate with some of what I did read. My writings are honest and unique to my experience. If I did not compile all of what I have endured, anorexia stays hidden. Hopefully my thoughts and perceptions can add a fresh twist on this terrible disease that affects more than just the host. You will never hear my words from the media because they will not dive into the complexities of anorexia nervosa. My writings aim to heal as I aim to continue doing the same....

My Scarlet Letter

Dedications
(Written when I was at my lowest point both physically and emotionally)

To my brother, Brian, I am sorry for making you anxious or that I ever judged you as anything but the best, sweetest, most compassionate guy I ever knew. To know that my disease affected you negatively upsets me greatly. You should not have had to deal with that interference. Know that I never meant for that to happen and know that you deserve every happiness. I love you.

To my sister, Kristen, I know it was hard for you to separate the parental and sister/friend parts of me. But I have always been and will always be your sister. Our family dynamics gave me an additional role that caused some friction. I am sorry for this and for the aggravations my disease has caused you. I know how much it sucked and my problem should have only affected me. It was not fair and I wish I could take back all of the resulting anger and pain. I hope that as you o forward in life, you will preserve that creative, infallible spirit that I love about you. Each day will be better knowing you do not have to deal with my craziness in the house anymore. I apologize that our sister bond got damaged by my demons,

My Scarlet Letter

but know that it will never be broken. We are sisters always and you are my pumpkin. Just remember that.

To my mother: I wish I could erase all the inevitable scars left on your heart. How tiring and overwhelming it must have been for you to deal with me. My disease needed to consume only me, not you. You have your own life to live and were in your own journey of rediscovery and rejuvenation. I should not have suffocated that inspiring journey. I never wanted to hinder that process for you and for that, I am very sorry. I hope you know I would never choose to do that to my most compassionate supporter. You saved me from an earlier checkout date, for sure. For this, I remain gratefully in your debt. I hope you can bury your heartache with me and move forward, living the happiest life you can imagine. Just think, no more questioning what you ate! Can you imagine the freedom you will feel without my voice grilling you? (Certainly a positive to look forward to). Now you can know that I am now free to be the real me, the daughter you missed for these three years or so, who will be with you always. I don't want to be thought of as a lost cause or that sad, sickly young woman. Please remember the true individual you know I was... even if you have to rewind to find positives, please do.

My Scarlet Letter

1

Absolute

    Standing in line at the grocery store and scanning the headlines, I tried so hard to separate myself from the stories. "Nicole Richie hits 90 lbs" or "Angelina won't eat, Brad worried" suddenly became echoes in my mind and with every glance at these covers, I felt everyone around me staring. I would read the articles and look at the pictures, comparing myself in terms of health. I would think, "I don't look as bad as they do" and be proud of that fact. I needed to lose weight anyways, so my sudden loss was initially a positive thing for me. I looked healthy in the beginning and I was not even exercising a lot, just walking. I was not eating perfectly healthy because, after all, I was in college. But somehow the combination worked. Slowly, I began to eat less and less and it did not take long for great to move to gaunt.

    I suppose what is so perplexing is that I was in my twenties when it hit me. This shit is supposed to happen in high school or college, if at all. So why did this happen? And to me, of all people. I was the first one to look at a sickly looking model on a magazine cover and say, "Eat a cookie." To me, these women were so vain and sucked into this

My Scarlet Letter

twisted competition with each other on who could reach skeletal first. It continues to be a hideous look for anyone, but societal pressures play a huge role. Everything I knew about anorexia nervosa was about young girls who were very skinny who would look at themselves in the mirror and say how fat and ugly they were. They called themselves names and had huge body image issues. Health was never a concern, because they were proud of either not eating, purging or exercising to burn off the few calories consumed. But there is such a fine line between all of this because, in my opinion, there are a lot more women with eating disorders than without one. Skipping meals is a common practice. But with me, it started subtly. There was never a day in my life where I said, "OK, I am going to stop eating now." Nor did I ever look in the mirror and think that I was a fat, ugly pig when I had already lost too much weight. It is the weirdest phenomenon and one that I'm not sure you can understand unless you have been there. And even then, each story is different. I cannot stress that enough, it is an extremely personal, individual struggle. I cannot say I have the ultimate, supreme answer, but I have an inkling.

When I reflect on who I am, I realize that I am a toxic combination of elements. What is surprising is that I made it this far in life without blowing a fuse or shutting down. But I prided myself in this strength and determination not to let anything get the best of me. I am quiet, by nature, and rarely yell. Everyone would tell me how calm and collected I was and how I had everything under control. What as

My Scarlet Letter

compliment! I was a rock. No crying, ever, because tears were weakness and I was not weak. I had trained myself not to show emotion. It was a sure sign of my restraint when my grandfather died and I would not let one tear come out at the funeral. I wanted everyone to know how strong I was because at least if I were a good person, no one would focus on my shortcomings. You could rely on me for anything and most people did. Why, just this past winter, I babysat my neighbor's eighteen-month old girl in the hallway of the hospital delivery room at 5 AM while her dad was in the emergency room for back pain and her mom was in labor about to deliver her beautiful baby brother. These neighbors had only been renting next door to me for about 6 months and we did not really know them that well, but somehow they knew I was a sucker for helping people out. There is nothing wrong with being a good person and I was happy to assist them in such stressful circumstances. The real problem was that it was affecting my own quality of life. My life and my needs were not as important as helping out other people. And that is a twisted way of existing.

Never was I "the pretty one", neither in school nor in my family. Always chubby and never a real athlete, I felt doomed to be anything but thin. Even when I would lose a few pounds, my frame was still larger than most. But I just accepted that fact and went about my merry way. I knew I was a good person and foolishly thought everything would work out. You know how your family tells you how pretty you are and how they would not change a thing about you

My Scarlet Letter

because you are special? Well, not everyone gets that message. My mother continues to tell me to just be happy with my body, but she has never been overweight in her life, except maybe during pregnancy. She was a cheerleader in high school and every guy lined up for her. Hell, my grandfather even caught one peeking in her window once. No boys ever lined up for me, but I knew that, in my family, that was to be my sister's destiny. Boys were already lining up for my sister when she was in middle school, but my line did not have any takers. Do not misunderstand me, I had a few guys interested and went out on the occasional date, but never anything like what I had dreamed about. Again, I settled and thought this was to be my life. I would continue trying to right everything that was going wrong in my family and friends' lives. It was not my job, but it felt like it was. I would feel terrible if I turned away, shrugged my shoulders and said, "Oh well." This was not me and the only thing I ever wanted in return was happiness. Now, I know life happens and you never know when your time is coming. But I let silly movies get to my head and delude reality. I would think, "Well, Drew Barrymore finally met the man of her dreams in her twenties in Never Been Kissed, so maybe I just need to be patient." It was not that I was not attractive enough; it just wasn't my time for everything to click. Boy, was I kidding myself, or what?

    Television and the media always made me feel less than a woman, but I knew I was not alone. I watched so many happy people go about their daily lives, taking for

My Scarlet Letter

granted how naturally thin and beautiful they were. They did not even have to try or, at least that is how it appeared. Hollywood starlets are attractive to begin with and then the glamour catches then and they get thinner to "help get roles". Only recently do we hear more about the struggles some faced with fitting the ideal image. Some still do not admit what lengths they have gone to for fame. As they say, denial is not just a river in Egypt; rather it is a state of mind that can last for decades. The word, anorexia, is such taboo and one is always quick to dismiss such an allegation because that would mean they would have to address it. Honestly, anorexia seemed like a joke before my own battle. It was a compliment to be thought anorexic. And people would joke about supermodels needing to eat more than a piece of lettuce. I believed these models to be vain and only care about perpetuating a mythical stereotype of beauty. And they were not eating on purpose. It was a sick, twisted competition and I was certainly not a part of it. I was not going to be taken by constantly being told I had to look like this. I know it was not an option and it was not reality. But more and more people succumbed to fad diets and deprivation tactics to achieve thinness and social acceptability. No matter what the damage was to the body, if you got thin you were beautiful.
This was not me, however.

    I know people who tried to get into the modeling business and were told to lose weight. I know people who, to me, are the perfect weight and look beautiful, yet they obsess

My Scarlet Letter

over scales and numbers. You cannot turn on the television or radio without an advertisement for some diet food or program coming on. Magazine headlines include something about weight and food every month! They promise to make you twenty pounds lighter in five days. Preposterous! But I was proud that I never tried these shortcuts. I felt sorry for celebrities who had to do this or, should I say, felt like they had to be tiny. Jessica Simpson got tormented for being, what, 125 pounds? She was 110 or something when she played Daisy Duke and it goes to show you it is not real. Unless you work out five hours a day and only eat about 500 calories, then it is not happening. Young girls in my classroom are already counting calories. I had a sixth grader who would not each her snack because it had too many calories and she was already, seventy-five pounds. My cousin's daughter was worried that her Wii Fit said she gained two pounds and she is in second grade. When you hear these stories, it is no wonder that so many succumb to eating disorders. You do not have to be full blown anorexic or bulimic to have an eating disorder. There are so many types of this disease. I see people skip meals and restrict themselves to less than the caloric intake your body needs to sustain bodily functions on a daily basis. I see people who obsessively over-exercise to burn off what they have had during the day. I have seen people only eat certain items, not because of allergies, but because of their diuretic effects on the body. But these types of cases go overlooked until the

My Scarlet Letter

weight drop and the behaviors start intensifying and affecting daily interactions.

"I do not think I am fat. I know I am too thin now. I have gone beyond a healthy, attractive lean look and am now sickly-looking. I do not call myself names and have celebrity bodies cutout and plastered around the house. I am not trying to be the thinnest and do not compare myself in such a way. People need to understand this is a myth...only true for some cases. No one realizes the power of this psychological disorder. I am 25 and I have anorexia nervosa. As I write these words, my throat seems to swell and I am full of shame in admitting such an embarrassing fact about me. It is a truth I never thought would be in my life or spoken from these lips..."

I am not an anomaly in terms of the restrictive behaviors of this disease. My suspicion is that more suffer than we know of because not everyone gets to the point of diagnosis or treatment. After my experience, I have noticed the habits of others more than ever and I see some alarming behaviors that I want to expose. The fact that I was called out and forced to address mine angers me. Why is it okay for everyone else to do it? Why is everyone on my case? Looking at pictures, I know I looked sick, but still it bothers me. There is such a fine line between a healthy and an unhealthy obsession.

To this day, there is a old man who goes to my favorite ice cream place and airs his car out every Saturday in the good weather. He is definitely OCD as he systematically opens

My Scarlet Letter

every door, including hood and trunk, and then sits inside staring at his car from the window. He never buys ice cream, just brings coffee and the paper and mumbles to himself when he stands by his car. Then he closes everything up and moves his car to another parking space (backing it in) and only opens the hood and trunk, no doors this time. It is bizarre to see, but it is his reality. There is something familiar, comfortable and necessary about this routine for him.

The difference in my case is that I started to show it in my appearance in a more dramatic way. If, as a teenager, I weighed only 125 pounds then it would not be quite as noticeable. You would see a difference, but no one would suspect anything until I started looking skeletal. So I was already a standout because I was never, ever thin. I was always chubby. So many people skip meals, but it is seem as normal. When I did it, I was branded as restricting. The human body needs 2,000 calories to function properly each day. But, by my calculations, the thin women do not eat that many calories. But for whatever reason, society accepts and condones restrictive behavior until someone gets sick or hurt. If you eat a whole sandwich, you are a pig. If you eat a piece of chocolate or even a bagel, you are a blob. It is almost a cultural badge of honor these days if you can get by on a salad and a piece of fruit a day. Your body gets used to not being nourished and starts to use itself for food. No one tells you about how "starvation mode" screws up your metabolism. Would we listen? Deep down, don't we all just

My Scarlet Letter

want to look good? Don't lie. It may not be your number one priority in life and some people do not attempt to change themselves due to depression and other factors, yet no one can deny that they enjoy looking a certain way. But, man, they do not tell you about the long-term effects on your body.

"The media is full of lies. They give us a picture and interpret their view only and no one else's. Usually, we never hear the truth, just another rumor and another headline. Well rumors were flying about me. My mother would shut herself in her room and cry on the phone to her friend. And I would hear her talking on the phone to her brother, who works at a hospital, trying to figure out what she could do for me. I hated hearing this. Deep down I was glad she cared, but on the surface I was so aggravated that she would not just leave me alone. "Did you eat? Want to come sit with us and have dinner? We will have whatever you what." This disease made me a liar. I always lied and said I had eaten. When I was included in dinner, I usually took my plate in the living room or somewhere out of site. I would wrap food in napkins and conceal them in the trash. If someone came around to check and see if I was eating, I would just put the napkin under the pillow or something. Even when I had my bowl of ice cream, that I really did eat, I built a wall of blankets and pillows and would stop eating if someone was peeking into my space from behind the couch. All you hear about in the media is celebrities just not eating at all or going on some ridiculous liquid diet. Is there ever any talk about the behaviors or emotion of the person besides a headline

My Scarlet Letter

about depression or being a zombie? I am much more interested in the ones that try and pretend like it is all okay and that is what I tried to do."

These routines of restriction come from the media in conjunction with those around us. Mothers with eating disorders are setting a poor and dangerous example for their children. A young girl is not going to eat more, especially when her mom is trying to keep her from gaining weight. Then there is the element of competition. No one wants to be the "fat one" in the family and stand apart from the slender counterparts. Consequently, no girl wants to be the least attractive in a group of friends. There are so many hidden pressures working against a healthy attitude about your body. Because of all of the above plus my own experience, I know I will never have the attitude I desire. My hope is to get to a point where I tolerate my body. I will accept it for its flaws and know it is a part of my being for as long as I am here. But I cannot see myself loving my body. I do not shut out the possibility, but it is so difficult to imagine. After all of my personal hell, I hope it will happen. I really do… but I am a glass-half-empty girl by nature.

I never truly fit into any stereotypical group. I was almost a year younger than my peers due to my birthday being a day or two before the cutoff. Why, then, have I always felt older than them? I look young, but my mind has always been displaced and disconnected with where I was in age. I always felt responsible, like a parent, but it was more than this fact. I find myself thinking about life's seemingly

My Scarlet Letter

impossible questions and pondering what others seemed to ignore. So where did I fit? I could pretend fairly well, I think, and could control emotions and thoughts so as not to single myself out in a crowd. All the while, I was searching and searching. I was doing what I was supposed to, when I was supposed, how I was supposed to, but I did not know why. Was I the only one who didn't get it? I would read magazines and watch movies, the same as any typically developing child, but it was not my reality. I believed that it was everyone else's world and I was a visitor who never left.

My Scarlet Letter

Forgotten
© 2007

Never thought of by friends.
A few close ones would be nice.
Never the first you'd call
Except for a listener
Never come to my side
Unless for personal gain
Your vast radar
Never registers my presence.
Soon after, even the airbag
Never knew I was there.

My Scarlet Letter

Besides the media, we, as a people, have been programmed into believing that thinness equates to happiness and beauty. Again, this was never me. When I started to lose weight and become thin, it was a problem. Few were happy for me looking better than before. When I switched from the fat one to the skinny one, I was accused of having a problem. At first, there was none. I was simply dropping some pounds. But when I became 'the skinny one' in the family, it was a role reversal that was not handled well. My family was used to me being a bigger girl. They were comfortable with it. So as I started to change, they started to question. I was not obsessing over food or calories or numbers, in the beginning. But all of the hyper-focus on me caused me to obsess over the situation. Now that I was thinner, I had to stay that way so that no one would make even more comments. I was paranoid with what people were saying and hate whispers and gazes. Outside of my family, people assumed I went on a fad diet or something extreme. My cousin told me, recently, that she knew I was in trouble, but her mother and aunt just thought I was dieting with no cause for alarm. Honestly, I did not hear an alarm for quite some time.

My Scarlet Letter

Untitled © 2009

You pace.
You worry.
You cry.

I support.
I am there.
I try.

You're in need
You're overwhelmed.
You're stressed.

I want to fix it.
I assist.
I obsess.

You fixate.
You exaggerate.
You can't move on.

Still I try.
Still I give.
Until it's gone.

My Scarlet Letter

Have you ever seen the movie 'Being John Malkovich'? It parallels my experience in an oddly coincidental kind of way. It is as if some evil force has infiltrated a portal into my body, controlling me and forcing decisions to be made that are not "real me" choices. True, the movie is more about the chance to be another person for fifteen minutes and truly walk in their shoes. But the main character, a puppeteer, learns how to control John Malkovich in such a way that he eliminates the separation of the two beings. Malkovich's body is simply a vessel, just a warm body. His mind and body become an experiment of control for the protagonist. He was not satisfied with who he was in his own life, so he took advantage of the situation to create the life he had always wanted.

On the outside, everyone knew Malkovich as Malkovich, even though he had changed. Only a few knew the truth, but the protagonist's power and control of the mind and body nearly eviscerated any trace of the real John Malkovich. Now, I know I have some control over myself, but it gets to a point where I can feel a force holding me captive. I become exhausted from trying to break free of this grasp. My soul and my spirit are thinking proactively, but my mind is sending mixed signals that never reach my limbs. There is a disturbance- someone is screwing with my wires and knotting my insides and I cannot stand it. They delight in my torment. So where is the strength to overcome it? I try to find peace, serenity and believe in the power of positive thinking. Yet people are dying suddenly of heart attacks and

My Scarlet Letter

strokes and I could just as easily drop dead. I know I am not going to grow old. Since elementary school, I felt like I was going to die young. And my body is in such agony. I am restless and fatigued. It is true, you know, the more control you feel you have, the less in control you actually are. I worry about everything. I control what I put in my mouth and compare it to others. I do not want to eat more than others. Ironically, in my current situation, I absolutely have to."

  I was not proud of what my appearance became, but I was sadistically proud of my restrictive behavior. I would keep tabs on what everyone was eating and marvel at the fact that I could quell my hunger and just not eat. Ironically, the thinnest face I had was devoid of the beauty that celebrities had. Tabloids would ream a model or someone for looking sickly and then the next week, they are on the "Best Dressed" list looking like a coat rack. Why is our society so fickle? I knew I was looking thin and everything I wore looked terrible. Yet, magazines and movies make us so desensitized to how thin is too thin. Once you lose too much weight, you lose more of your identity because all frail, thin frames look alike. Curves and shape give you a presence. I see that now, and not many of us appreciate it. I remember seeing the movie Chicago and looking at Renee Zellweger's elbows thinking they just didn't look right. She was pale and boney, yet desirable to movie producers. Catherine Zeta Jones, on the other hand, was a healthy, beautiful woman who looked huge next to Renee. In reality, however, Jones was more

My Scarlet Letter

attractive. She was by no means fat, but you could not help but notice the difference between the two on the stage. Did Zellweger need to lose that much for the role? No. She would have been find with an extra ten or fifteen pounds on her. Still thin, but at least she would have a little more to her body.

  Our bodies are not built for such abuse. Eventually, they will give us a message. If we are lucky, we will hear it and heed the warning. Most will be too vain and continue unhealthy practices and ride that roller coaster. I did not get in line for the ride. I walked with a few people and ended up roaming around the crowd. Somehow, without my realizing it, I ended up in line and on the first car. Yet I do not remember wanting to go on the ride in the first place. I remember thinking that looks a little too unsettling to me. I am going to hang out on my own and wait for others to get off. At this point, I lost myself to the negative thoughts and self-destructive routines. I felt as if I were poisoned and brainwashed. The thoughts were not mine, an outside force imposed them. People who knew me struggled to find evidence of me buried deep, deep in this prison.

  "I am horrified each time I step into the shower. I look so bizarre and so unreal. I feel like I am a character, a puppet controlled by a dark, evil force. I have no chest, no butt, no fat pads in my cheeks and no definition or curves. You can practically see a 360-degree view of my entire collarbone and my elbows are severely concave at the bend. My veins pop out on my hands and arms like someone on

My Scarlet Letter

steroids. I can actually see the ones on the back of my hands move around like a live power wire fallen from a pole undulating on the ground and, man, does it feel weird. I cannot sit because my bones hit every chair and it hurts like hell. Imagine sitting on two rocks and trying to move back and forth to find a spot that is not painful for more than thirty seconds. My eye sockets are sunken and I look gaunt. If I were proud of being skinny, I would have no problem going to my friend's wedding reception. But I cannot go looking like this. I would look terrible in any dress. I wore an extra small a year ago to a different wedding (and I weighed more then). So I am a horrible friend because I cannot go and be an eyesore. She will think I don't care. But I don't want to ruin her special moment. What if I pass out or something? No. I cannot go. I wish this disease did not affect absolutely everything."

  Perhaps this poisonous infection correlates to what happened to a celebrity. At one point in their lives, they were human. But then fame and fortune tempts them and they not only bite the apple, they consume it in its entirety. Soon they just start to behave differently and, lose their grasp on their former reality. The new reality is more like virtual reality as it is not necessarily tangible. I have never been famous, so I am just hypothesizing. Yet, it does make sense. We love to think that we are our own people, individually, and we live above the influence, but it is a lie. Everyone is influenced. No one can escape that fact.

My Scarlet Letter

    Even in elementary school, your foundation of knowledge is based on what books that school used. Your alphabet associations will depend on what alphabet strip was scrolling around your classroom. If A is for apple, it will never be for airplane. If green is the grass, it cannot be broccoli. When I say something is blue, is it what you would consider blue, too? Are my eyes seeing what your eyes see? How do I know that everyone sees the same colors? I guess it doesn't matter, because everyone agrees to agree that the sun is yellow and the sky is blue. We question why the sky is blue but not why is an apple red? I have never seen an apple as red as school-related books and bulletin board decorations. Red delicious apples do not look like that. Even Macintosh apples are not uniformly bright red. Yet, when it comes to beauty, there is also a standard taught in this hidden curriculum of our culture.

    As early as the toddler years, we are muttering the word "pretty" because we would hear it when wearing a dress or when we had to look special for something. Then we start to pay more attention when we hear the word and watch who is saying and it to whom. Then "beautiful" is spoken and we connect that word with whom we hear and see it spoken to by another. Consequently, we notice who it was not said to and who is never referred to as this word. Simple? Seemingly insignificant? Maybe. But there is an impact. Even a small impact compounds over time and, sometimes, can escalate into misconceptions and feelings of inadequacy, which lead to physical and psychological issues. The power

My Scarlet Letter

of the mind is not something to be taken lightly, for its complexities continue to transform on a daily basis.

It is this very phenomenon that made anorexia what it is in our culture today. It is not discussed as a psychological suicide where the sufferer has no regard for his/her own body or life, in general. We do not hear about the severe emotional pain and torturous agony of each day, each hour and each breath. Instead, we hear about the vanity of it-the desire to be thinner. Thin equals beauty and anorexics are simply people who wanted to be thin, took it too far and cannot come back. This is what we are told and this is what we grow up thinking is the truth because nothing has challenged that notion. Anorexia still seems to be a joke in society...just something to gawk at and use in a monologue on late-night television.

My Scarlet Letter

2
Analytical

"They tried to make me go to rehab, I said no, no, no!"

I'm sure you know of this Amy Winehouse song that seemed to get popular around the time I was really suffering. My mother would turn it up anytime it came on the radio in the car. I could not believe the timing of this song's popularity. I felt like each time it was on television or radio that people were looking at me. It was as if it was a song just for me. I hated the idea of going to rehab and I was determined to stay away. I did, however, write a letter to my mother stating that I would go into a program if I was not on the mend by my next birthday. I signed it and had her sign it, too. I wanted her to know that I was capable of trying. I could feel myself trying to make sense of things in my head. I knew I was not giving up, but no one else could see that. The force in my brain was so strong; it was controlling virtually every part of me. I would have moments of clarity where I would think, "Stop! You are still in control. Don't give in. Do not give up, Jen" But there were so many voices of negativity that silenced that one voice of hope. These voices strangled my will and my hope to the point of exhaustion. "Look at what you are doing to everyone. Look at how happy they are when you are back here and not sitting

My Scarlet Letter

down with them. See how everything you say makes everyone upset. Why do you think you deserve to eat? You make everyone miserable." This was constant. I was a slave to this parasitic disease, but I was attempting to move as forward as I could with my adult life.

    In 2005, I was a student at Lesley University studying for my Master's degree in education. Before enrolling, I worked the holiday season at Crate & Barrel. The discount was great, but the hours sucked. I was a floor stocker, going back and forth to the stock room and filling displays. There was this one guy, in his forties at least, who was always talking to me like we were best buds. The weird thing was that I mentioned being an artist and gave him a postcard. He said he was an accountant and could help with taxes if a sold a lot of art and needed to file. That was fine and I didn't mind talking to him at work.

    But after the job stopped, I got a random phone call from him asking how I was doing. So I felt really awkward and wanted the conversation to be over. And then he started asking if he could "take care of me" and how he'd like to "take care of me" if I'd let him. What the hell did that mean? I said, "No, I'm good thanks." But he persisted and said what a great person I was ad he loved talking to me and I was really sweet. In my mind, I am screaming. Is this guy for real? Could someone my age please be interested in me? I always get crazy stalker-type people. He called multiple times and I told my family not to answer the phone because an older guy with hair that was swiftly moving to grey is

My Scarlet Letter

pursuing me. I was freaked out. Flashbacks to childhood started playing in my mind.

When I was probably six or seven, my second cousin (my great aunt's son) used to offer to buy me a parrot. I never wanted a bird but when I visited my Auntie Peggy, her son with a raspy voice and the scent of cigarette smoke would joke about taking me away from my parents. He said I was a sweet kid and he was going to kidnap me. Of course, this was all in jest, but to a young kid it feels real. I didn't want to go visit when he was there because he would say that my mom and dad better watch out because he wanted to keep me. Now, he had his own kids, but I think he had no filter and no tact about what he was saying. I think most people found it amusing, but I kept thinking to myself, "I cannot live with this guy. I don't know him and I don't like birds." Even as I got older, he referred to me as "the one he wanted to steal" so I guess I am doomed for weird interactions with older men.

When the holiday season ended, so did my time at that job and I felt that Lesley was going to be a good place for me. I had a direction and felt confident I was going to be a certified art teacher and, hopefully, have a steady job. As I began my student teaching, I was also taking 14 credits worth of classes on top of that. So I would be in Peabody Monday through Friday until 3:00 or so and then drive to Cambridge for a 4-7 class on Monday, Wednesday, and Thursdays. Tuesdays I had a 7-10 class in Kenmore Square. On those nights, I would not get home until about 11.

My Scarlet Letter

Occasionally, I did a studio course on Friday as well. So I should have scaled back a class or two while teaching, but I am an overachiever and wanted to get everything done. At this time, I was also seeing someone and my father was moving out. At first, I thought I was going to have a person to spend quality time with and someone who cared for me, for a change. But, as it turned out, I was the only thoughtful one in the relationship. I am cursed with this obligation to help others and put myself last. Having a boyfriend, I thought, would balance it out, as he would be thinking of me, too. But was I ever wrong. Some guys are just not good partners and continue to be selfish and immature when it comes to relationships. And, as much as I hate to refer to clichés, guys really do only want one thing. When I was not willing to have a relationship purely based on physicality (and he did not want to be there for me emotionally), he could not handle it. He may have cared about me, but it was rare and in trace amounts. I moved on from this disappointment and really focused on finishing my degree with a renewed sense of purpose. I began to feel that I really could be a great teacher and bring passion and warmth to each student.

  I made some friends and, despite the stress of the classes, I enjoyed it. I am a lifelong learner and thrive in challenging situations. But, as my parents began with the divorce procedures and I was approaching my final semester, my weight loss became more noticeable. I remember at the opening for our thesis show, one of my classmates asked me

My Scarlet Letter

if I was alright or if I was sick. Then I met up with one of my professors and talked pretty much through the meal and had only taken a few bites. She mentioned something about talking care of myself and not getting too overwhelmed. So here I was thinking that I had it all under control and, I did, for the most part. I was going to graduate with a near 4.0 GPA and had a job lined up for the fall.

Yet, due to bouncing around from place to place, I would stay away from home if there was not enough time in-between classes or meetings. I wanted to stay in the zone, so to speak. And, remember, I believed my presence was a poison, so I would park my car by the lake, the beach or even a random parking lot and just walk around. Sometimes I just sat in my car with the heated seat cranking. But most of the time, I was researching for a lesson, picking up something for teaching or working on one of my numerous projects. Did I have to do it? No. I could have done just fine without the extra efforts. Yet, the hyper-focus brought an odd calming to my mind, as I knew I had the best intentions. I was exhausted, but no one could call me lazy or lacking in determination. And, I could not complain about shedding the extra pounds. I was not dieting, just not eating enough during the day. It was nice to not stand out as the chubby one, but I was not actively pursuing the weight loss. Grad school was demanding and I demand a lot of myself, in general.

Upon completing my degree, my mom had a big party at a hall in my honor. While it was nice of her, I definitely

My Scarlet Letter

did not want the spotlight on me. I was proud of my accomplishments, but ashamed of my frail appearance. At this party would be family and friends who knew me in a healthier state and they will spend the time talking about how sick I look and not about what I have done.... or at least not to my face. I wanted to celebrate, but could not enjoy any of it. My father's side of the family, in particular, loves gossip. I remember seeing my father's aunt and cousin at the store months before my party and they commented on the weight loss. My great aunt had a disgusted look on her face as her daughter told me that she "wasn't going to visit another person in the hospital." At the time, her cousin was in the hospital after a heart attack. So I smiled and went on my merry way after that heartwarming encounter. There was no kindness in them, just basically a tone like "wise up, girl". So I dreaded seeing them at my party. I knew everyone was going to come, not to celebrate me, but to check up on me and see how ugly I looked. Can you believe these were my thoughts about a party in my honor? My college roommate was coming as well as my practicum supervising teacher and a few other friends.

It was a rainy evening on party night and my father insisted on helping to setup easels for my artwork (another distraction for people). I had put a lot of thought into the centerpieces, which were table easels with art quotes on them. I got blue pencil with orange writing made with the text "make your mark". At the entrance, I put a canvas and a guest book. Most people signed their names on the canvas

My Scarlet Letter

and a few brave ones sketched on it. All of these details made a nice event, but there was still this awkward presence in the room. My mother made me come to the middle of the dance floor for the cake and to read a lovely paragraph she wrote about me. Subconsciously, she was trying to make me feel better about myself so I would want to live longer and not let myself die.   Neither of us ate dinner that night. She was "busy" circulating and avoiding it, in my opinion. I, too, circulated but you would expect that because I was the one suffering with the disease. To complicate the situation, one of the waitresses had taken a liking to me. She kept coming up to my friends saying, "Make sure she eats, okay?". She also enjoyed my artwork and started to tell me about her love of drawing. Along with that was her suggesting that I model for one of her drawings. My jaw dropped and I said, "No thanks, I am more comfortable in front of the canvas than behind it." But she was persistent and found ways to cross my path and make eyes across the room. Great, more awkwardness in the room, as if it could be any more tense in there.

"So, do you see your father?" was another comment by a great uncles who always says and does as he pleases. He even looked through my mother's closets when she had an open house years ago. "Sometimes..." was my response. But he would continue, "You don't look well. You need to eat something."

"Thank you. I have to go greet a few more people." I mean, this is my graduation party, a celebration.... supposedly.

My Scarlet Letter

Granted, I was more analytical than excitable, but I wanted to at least pretend I could have a good time without worrying over and over and over. I had some friends there and, of course, no one said anything about how I looked. But I found myself embarrassed to sit at the same table. They ate and I got up and went to walk around. I watched my mother intently as she, too, avoided eating the meal for which she had paid. Later that night, when we got home, I told her that she had not eaten anything and she ate a piece of cake because her excuse was being "too busy hosting". But, for some reason, that reason never flew when I used it. Anyone else could skip a meal without comment, but not me.

    Looking back at the pictures, I understand why it was a huge focal point. But I cannot tell you how much it hurt when my family deliberately avoided food conversations. It was my party, and I was so stressed that my teeth were clenching and I thought my head would explode. It was torture to be around so many people. My mother even made a speech so that I had to step out in front of everyone. Her expression of love and pride was beautiful and I wanted to really enjoy the moment in the way it should have been enjoyed. She got emotional and, in a way, I think it was almost a eulogy. She spoke about my accomplishments and, deep down, I think she believed it may be her last opportunity to do so. I was "visibly anorexic" and everyone just existed around me. I was alive, but not living. I was there, but might as well be at home. I felt that people came under obligation, not love or support. But, I got up and

My Scarlet Letter

hugged my mom and thanked her for her love, but I wished I could just be a fly on the wall and not have so many eyes judging me all at once. It was such a difficult night. My college roommate slept over and drove back home the next morning. Before leaving, we went to Dunkin Donuts for breakfast. She had breakfast and I had nothing. I sat there knowing I should have eaten, but the fear and internal anguish was paralyzing.

    This night was supposed to be for me but all I could do was obsess. It truly felt like a living funeral, complete with my father hovering and lingering in the shadows and not showing any emotion, as per usual. I saw myself being weird and pretending to be normal around my friends and could not stop the chain reaction. People greeted my and congratulated me on graduating and then avoided me like the plague. I believed everyone to be checking their watches under the table, desperately hoping for it to be time to make a departure from this suffocating room.

    At this point, I was still in denial of any issue forming. And I got a job before graduation, so I was psyched! I was going to be an art teacher for real and wanted to make sure I gave two hundred percent! Amid all of my hard work, I got rundown. There were days where I would struggle to keep my eyes open in meetings. I think I nodded off once, but my assigned school mentor approached me during my second year of teaching to inform me that people are concerned about me, just so I would know. What do you do with that information? Ok, I am fine, thanks. But after my scary

My Scarlet Letter

allergic reaction that landed me in the emergency room, I had to tell the school nurse about it. Now, I did not have many real friends in the building, so I am positive people were talking about me. I had an apple and some kashi cereal in the teacher's room occasionally and the gym teacher always asked me if I was still hungry. "Do you eat like this on the weekends, too?" So when I told the nurse I may need to get an epi pen, she was shocked and asked to be kept informed. She only cared because if something happened at school, she needs to know. But I knew no one in the building cared about me. They knew I was a good artist and, so far, a good teacher. No one could speak ill of me because I made no waves.

     I can remember one day during my second year of teaching when I felt so exhausted on my drive to work. My eyelids were so heavy and my head was bobbing. I had the radio turned up and shouldn't have had the heat on, but I needed it. Without warning I heard three loud car horns, Beep! Beep! Beeeeeeep! I lifted my head and turned to look out my passenger side window and this woman was mouthing the words, "Wake up!" to me with a look of anger and disgust. I was so startled and ashamed. How long was my head down? Did I swerve? Oh God, what am I doing? I was so shaky, but somehow made it to school and told no one. My jitters had subsided and my heart felt heavy and slow. I knew that brachycardia meant less than sixty beats a minute, so I timed myself and put two fingers on my wrist. Thump....thump........................thump..........th-thump............

My Scarlet Letter

Fifty-three by my count. But that is close enough to sixty, right? Let's try again. This time hand over chest. Hmm, not really too strong a beat to count here. Other wrist then.
... Thump.... thump.................thump....
thump........................thump
Dull beats and a slow breath. No other pains, but I was getting scared. I was swallowing to make sure my airway was clear and making myself breathe rather than to feel the natural rhythm. So I was debating on whether or not to go have to nurse take my blood pressure. Finally, I went to ask the principal if someone could cover my classes, as I was not feeling well. She sat me down and asked what was wrong and I said I might be coming down with something because I was feeling kind of lightheaded and my chest was tight. She asked if I wanted the nurse to check me out and I did not want to make a spectacle, I just wanted to go home and rest. She said she would feel better if the nurse got a reading before letting me drive home. What could I do? She agreed to send the nurse to her office and not to have me go to down to the nurse so kids would not see me. In came the nurse with her stethoscope and blood pressure band. I was so incredibly nervous as I pulled up my sleeve and let the cool air hit my bony elbow and watched her wrap the band around my arm and try to make it tight. I could not hide this. The reading was going to be whatever it is. She said my blood pressure was quite low and checked my heartbeat, too. Her concerned face is one I could not soon forget. She recommended I go to the doctor and get checked out, but I

My Scarlet Letter

just wanted to be home. They both asked me if everything was alright and they have noticed me not looking well. The principal said, "You were not that big when I hired you, but you have gotten a lot smaller since then. I know whatever is going on is your business but, with your age, you could be my daughter. I want you to know we will check in on you like your mothers at work. We are worried about you." I thought to myself, well of course you are, you don't want me to drop right here. But I did think they were nice to express concern, though I was so embarrassed. Now I was vulnerable.

    I can remember the moment I could no longer deny that I had a problem. My mother drives a Lexus with lovely features like heated leather seats and a steering wheel that moves to your preset settings. In addition, she has the more common flashing red seatbelt light when either she or her passenger does not have the belt on. To the left of that, there is a light that I had not seen before this day, a light that is never on. The light reads "Airbag off" and usually pops on when no one is sitting in the passenger seat so that it would not deploy when my mother has no passenger or had a child in the front. My mother had assumed I was doing better with going to therapy and starting with a nutritionist, by she gave me such a stare when I got into her car and that light stayed on. Initially, I tried to move around and press my butt down as hard as I could to get the light to go off. After that day, it occasionally worked until I was no longer just a couple of pounds off of the limit. The light stayed on if there was less than a hundred pounds on the seat. Clearly, I was

My Scarlet Letter

less but I refused to admit it. I told my mother the scale indicated otherwise, but she knew I could not deny it. As I got worse, a case of water on my lap was not turning that damn light off.

    I was lying about what food I ate. I was always in another room pretending to eat. I would pack food into napkins and put them inside folded paper plates, if possible. I would walk into a room where my mother or sister would be sittings and chew on the inside of my cheeks to simulate chewing real food. I thought I was being convincing, but they knew better. And, though I thought I could keep up the charade, I was only becoming more conspicuous in my behaviors.... it was absolutely terrible. I felt like my grandmother, who is currently slipping into the early stages of Alzheimer's and is aware of her lack of memory and word recollection, except I was painfully aware of actions I could not stop.

    My mother and I have been taking my grandmother out on the weekends for years to get an ice cream at Richardson's, run errands and give my grandfather a break. I would order the dishes and sit in the back, slowly scraping away little spoonfuls. From there, I started to order my mother ice cream instead of frozen yogurt and always acted as if the server made the error. If I had to eat, she was going to have the ice cream. But I began to spit my mouthfuls out in the napkins as I huddled behind my grandmother in the passenger seat. (Like my mother could not see me in the mirror.) I would have a stack of napkins with melting frozen

My Scarlet Letter

yogurt on the floor until I took everyone's trash to the barrel. (Ridiculous, I know.) And, as if I could not find a way to make it even more bizarre, I started getting frappes and would simply suck halfway up the straw, or just until the drink reached my lips and fake a swallow. I never truly took a normal sip and, because, I took care of walking the trash to the barrel, I assumed I was outsmarting them. This was my routine and I could not bring myself to stop being so weird about food. I remember one time that my brother came, sat next to me in the backseat and I STILL packed away the napkins! What was I thinking?! Of course, my brother did not know what the hell to do, so he said nothing and ignored me. Imagine what he must have been thinking about me. No, I would rather not know how low his opinion of me must have dropped that day.

When I add days like that to my behavior at holidays and any other family gathering, I shudder to think about what must have been going through everyone's minds. At the first "poisoned" Thanksgiving, we went to my cousin's house where her husband, two kids, mother, father, aunt and brother were in addition to my father, brother and sister. I remember helping in the kitchen eighty percent of the time. As soon as I got there, I was asking what I could do. I mashed potatoes, heated up the gravy and the stuffing, got everyone a drink and spooned the components of their meal into their respective dishes. I waited until the last possible minute to join the table and, when I did, I put mostly vegetables on my plate and drank a glass of water very

My Scarlet Letter

slowly. Potatoes, stuffing, cranberry sauce, rolls, green beans and carrots were being passed around the table and, when they came to me, I continued to pass. My sister glared out of the corner of her eye and my uncle joked about my plate. After about twenty minutes of the charade, I would jump up and start cleaning up for the remainder of the meal. I enjoyed it and did not mind doing it. I do, however, realize the avoidance, but I am always the helper no matter where I am.

   The next Thanksgiving I do not believe I sat down at all. My uncle and father began eating before everyone because of the football games. So, it was not as if we were even all eating a communal meal, as Thanksgiving should be. Therefore, while everyone else sat down to eat, I collected the plates from the boys and started to clean and refill any low bowls of mashed potatoes. I was really hoping no one would bring up the fact that I was not sitting down. I planned to tell them I ate leftovers while working at the counter. But, again, no one seemed bothered by it except my sister who would often get in my face and ask what I ate and when. She would get disgusted when I would lie and then watch to make sure she ate something. I watched as she ate modestly and no one made a comment. It was so unsettling to me. The headaches were the worst on holidays and birthdays. Even today, my holidays are off. Now that I am recovering, I feel like everyone is watching me thinking, "She should not be eating those potatoes" or just staring at the anomaly I am. I know some of this is in my own head, but it is so difficult to

My Scarlet Letter

get beyond in certain situations. People that did not know me at my worst do not have that memory of me engrained in their minds. But those who saw my downward spiral remain most difficult for me to be comfortable around. Of course, my immediate family was there to witness my suffering and it is guilt that I feel around them. I caused them so much pain and stress and I cannot get past that fact. I long for family gatherings to be warmer and to bring the joy they once did when I was a child. Even in college, holidays were special and anticipated. Now, they are met with dread and I despise this feeling. So this disease already robbed so many aspects of my life and now it had ruined my family holiday celebrations. Perhaps one day, I will rekindle that flame, as it should never have been extinguished. How sad is it that I have not eaten a piece of my own birthday cake in about five years? I am not sure when I will.

My Scarlet Letter

3
Anomaly

    I think sending me to Walden or Cambridge would be my mother's magic wand. Hell, she would put me on the A&E Show "Intervention" if she could. But the fact remains... anorexia nervosa is primarily an adolescent disease. Those who suffer in their twenties, thirties or forties usually started with a teenage eating disorder of some kind. I have read so many books and heard so many stories about adults who recall problems when they were younger and can chronicle the progression into adulthood. For me it had nothing to do with "the perfect body" and trying to be a supermodel. I watched "Intervention" and saw girls pinching their skin in front of the mirror and calling themselves "pigs" and wanting to look a certain way. I never did that and I loathed being compared to those girls. It was all a self-esteem issue for these girls and they needed to be comfortable with their bodies. I was never really comfortable as a teenager, but in college I accepted my body. I was lighter than I was in high school because I walked around campus a lot and made smarter food choices. I didn't need to be a size 2 and didn't care about being that small. I knew I could be happy being a size 10. Fitting into a large, occasionally a medium, was great with me. Therefore I could not follow a chronological path like others with the disease. I was not a dancer or gymnast where there was physical pressure in addition to the societal and social pressures.

My Scarlet Letter

    My mother worked hard to find me the best psychologist who specialized in eating disorders and, initially, I only went to appease her. When my mother confronted me and said she believed I had a problem, I thought she was reading into nothing. I believed she was creating an issue from a busy day-to-day life. After finishing my graduate work, I was throwing myself into my job. She told me I avoided mealtimes and stayed late at work in order to miss dinner. What? I was working my ass off to run a classroom and work out any kinks so I could be the best teacher possible. One or two classmates from Lesley asked if I was alright, but only once. Looking back at my graduation pictures, I am stunned that no one said more. If I were walking around with a broken leg, wouldn't someone say something? And a broken leg is far less serious than what was happening to me. My supervising practitioner saw no cause for alarm until she saw me a year later at Trader Joe's. She emailed me with concern but, by that time, I was too far into this disease.

    I dreaded going to therapy because she wanted information from me and kept asking me those questions that might be true for other anorexic girls, but not me. She kept asking about my calorie counting and if over over-exercised for hours to burn off everything. She clearly did not get it. My answers with her were short and she was frustrated, but always analyzing me as I was her. That was the friction, she quickly learned that I took everything thing in and knew she was trying to figure me out so I was not

My Scarlet Letter

offering any clues. It was this game where if I had to go to these sessions, at least I was going to plan ahead for them. I wanted to be prepared and think about all the different ways she was going to pull me and I was never going to show weakness, so good luck getting me to cry. I would go in and lie to her face about what I was eating. She and my mother had conspired against me and were making me sound horrible with all of my behaviors. That was not me! That was not what I wanted her to know about me!

"So my new patient, Jen, is withdrawn, not eating, always mad and negative to her family while watching everyone else's habits and looking in the trash. Oh, and she never sits down and has the personality of a pine needle."

It was like this news feed and I had no rebuttal, because it was one against everyone. It was so unfair. Even when I corrected something, she would make a face and pull her mouth to one side saying, "Oh…I see". I felt like screaming, "Stop judging me! You have no clue who the real me is and what this disease is twisting!!"

But if I did that, I would be coming twice a week. And insurance did not cover it, so I already felt guilty for my mother paying for the weekly torture. I felt weird, already, about how I was in this anorexic body, and, always knew I was weird in my former state.

But I would skip appointments and, when I did show up, I was so guarded and untrusting. I looked over her shoulder at the clock every chance I had. And when she would ask probing questions, I would have an internal battle

My Scarlet Letter

about what to disclose. Honestly, I did not want her knowing anything because she was only doing what she was paid to do and had no real investment into my life or me, as a person (not as an anorexic young woman). She was an expert in this field and would surely apply some theories to my situation and I felt the need to challenge her at every point.

    My psychologist talked to me as if I did not have a functioning brain anymore. I was not brainwashed. Rather, I was able to function and trapped inside this rusty cage full of fists that would beat on me every time I fought the downward spiral. She made me feel worse about myself, if that was even a possibility. I was alone and I had been bitten with incisors of obsession and poisoned with the venom of depression.

My Scarlet Letter

Square Peg
© 2009

Playground days
I was not alone
But never the same

Would play and talk
Cautiously, of course
Always worried

Thinking too much
About consequences
And responsibility

Not a free spirit
Far from carefree
Usually guilt or blame

Concerned for others
Even strangers
Odd as it seems

Could not let go
Remained a rock
No matter the day.

My Scarlet Letter

Never was trashed
Too much at stake
Too many to watch

But funny as can be
When truth breaks through
Yet pretending is the norm

What can be done?
Goodness eludes
Well, me, that is.

Others find it
In abundance
But it's hidden from me.

I don't understand,
Destined, I guess,
I continue to just be.

My Scarlet Letter

And as if therapy was not enough, I added on a nutritionist at the therapist's request. This was not simply a nutritionist; she was an eating disorder specialist at the hospital. (Great). Appointments at the hospital with a woman who would dissect my meals and force me to eat more. (How could I concoct a faux meal plan?). This added another layer of stress. She would think of me as an idiot, for sure. She will think that I am trying to idealize myself to a supermodel and think it is a self-esteem issue. Was she going to weigh me? Was I going to have to keep a journal? Was she going to send me into a program? Would she treat me like a child?

One the day of the first appointment, I pulled into the parking lot and sat in my car for about a half hour debating on whether or not to just leave. I had skipped therapy appointments before, but the therapist and nutritionist knew each other. They would surely talk. I managed to turn off my engine and walk slowly toward the entrance. Little did I know that I was going into the children's hospital, since this is where her office was and, let's face facts, it is a childhood issue for a majority of the population. So I was embarrassed to be there, of course.

"What are you here for?" the receptionist asked.

"I have an appointment at 4:00 with the nutritionist."

"Is it for you or do you have a daughter?" she continued.

"No, it's me." I answered.

My Scarlet Letter

"Oh, sorry. Do you have an insurance card?" I passed it across the desk along with my license. "I didn't look at the date, sorry about that. First door down the hall is her office. Knock first and give her this form."

I wanted out, but I was checked in now. Not only was I checked in, I was also at the door that was being opened for me and saw the seat I was to sit in. This was going to be painful. Aside from the tension, I would get these weird palpitations and, as I got weaker, I could feel each and every heartbeat and every inhalation and exhalation in my body. So when I was nervous, this sensations only got more intense and I always thought I would drop right there and that would be it. But, I reluctantly sat in the chair even though chairs and I did not get along at all. I could not sit on a wooden chair because my bony butt had no cushioning. Every time my body leaned, my bones were in direct contact with the chair. I was used to this everywhere I went and I think this contributed to my never wanting to sit. In my car, I would leave two imprints on the black leather, so each time I got up, you could see them. It was a bizarre sight.

But her chair was fabric and it was on one side of a table and her on the opposite side. My first thought was, "Great, another analyzer trying to get me to say certain things." She was part of what became known as my "team". I was skeptical from the first handshake. Again, I gave only one-word answers and lied through my teeth about how healthily I was eating on a daily basis. She was sided with my psychologist and would check in and report on me back

My Scarlet Letter

and forth. So how could I trust either of them? In hindsight, I know they had the best intentions, but I was convinced it was hopeless. I had lost my former life and could not find the person I knew I had always been. I was not evil. I was not crazy. Yet, there I was in the children's hospital waiting room month after month, thinking I was fooling everyone.

  I was going, so my mother would be pleased. She would hear that I was trying but that my body just was not gaining weight. Her psychologist talked to mine, too, because I was causing my mother so much pain right as she was going through a divorce. But my nutritionist was more blunt than my therapist. She came out with "Jen, you are killing yourself and you are going to die soon." one afternoon when we met. I could feel my heart racing and I was waiting to have my heart stop right then and there. She told me she detected the scent of ketones, which is an odor the body gives off when it is overproducing digestive juices, and is only picked up by trained nasal passages, I guess. I went home and washed everything in an attempt to get rid of the smell. But I loathed the shower. I was afraid I would collapse after peeling off all of my layers. I was so cold; my body would convulse each time a showered. It was painful and frightening, so I tried to do it less and less. I figured, I am not sweating, so I do not really need to do it that much.

My Scarlet Letter

"   After starting these appointments, I also sought alternative methods to break the vicious self-hatred. My mother's yoga instructor is a Reiki master and he believes he could help me detoxify my body and mind. I don't know much about the metaphysical theories, but Helen is obsessed with the whole realm of spirituality. After meeting him, I see where she gets her ideas. He talks about himself a lot, is quite blunt yet full of information. He, too, had an alcoholic father who was verbally abusive and sent him into a deep depression until he was 33 and yoga saved his life. It is about balancing the mind, body and spirit so that harmony can be achieved. I am in discord, desperately trying to find that balance. Never having meditated, it is difficult for me to access that level immediately. Paul could never cry before, but he does now. It is essential to the cleansing process. He tried to make me cry when I met with him for an hour, but I am too trained to hold it in and not release tears. But he cried for me and, consequently, the pain he felt through me. He said he saw hope in my left eye and my right eye (does not open as wide) is damaged. Coincidentally, I have an astigmatism in that eye. Supposedly the left is the female eye and the right is male.

    He performed a Reiki sequence on me, but I was not fully relaxed. He held different parts of my body and put crystals on the chakra zones. At first, I felt them heavily resting on me but, by the end, they were practically weightless. My hips were, apparently, like steel and all locked up in pain. He pressed on areas and tugged on my

My Scarlet Letter

ankles. Trust, anger and pain came up a lot. He told me I had a beautiful spirit and found no negative energy. (Ha! to my family). I focused of the deep cleansing breaths and he questioned and questioned. I ended up in the bow position taking short, rapid breaths that made me quite uncomfortable. My lower back and neck were killing me and it was like someone was pressing on my esophagus. I had to stop because I thought I was going to stop breathing. I tried it two or three more times to please him, but it still hurt. He informed me to project my pain into the pose, but all I could focus on was the discomfort. I guess it causes some people to cry or throw up. The next bow pose, holding my ankles, was not as bad. Getting out of it was harder than maintaining it. Lifting my chest and neck proved to be difficult. He suggested more B vitamins and gave me some energy elixir with bee pollen, ginseng, honey and pure royal jelly. I was to take the royal jelly twice a day because it is the strongest, most concentrated vitamin costing $50 and he sells them for $25. I got one for free to try. It is quite bitter and pungent, but I was willing to try it if it will strengthen me.

  I find it so compelling that I cannot express my anger. I cannot force yelling or screaming. Oddly enough, he had me swinging a bat yelling, "I hate you" and making grunt noises and yelling. The yells were pathetic because it is not me and I felt silly. He could see the anger, but could not make me give a heartfelt yell. But, man, could I swing that bat. My arms and thighs were sore when I left. He

My Scarlet Letter

thinks I should come to yoga and go at my own pace and I hope I will be able to do that. I need to put 5 pounds on by Halloween, for sure. If not, hospital here I come. As it was, I should have gained a pound by next week when I see the nutritionist. I should be 97 pounds, but my home scale says 94.5 with clothes and shoes. Without clothes, I range from 90.3 to 93 pounds. She knows the clothes add weight, but we'll see what happens. I have a week and I have to deal with dinner at the Hardcover and then Bertucci's I think and, yes, I am nervous."

My Scarlet Letter

Parallel
© 2008

Unsteady is my step,
The beat in my chest is slow,
My breath is voluntary and
There's no control of the urge to go.

Sunken and aged,
I do not recognize my face.
As I speak, I cannot
Back up my own case.

The words escape my lips
And my tongue tastes like tar.
I cannot even lift my own leg
To get into my own car.

Normal struggle, I suppose
For the older souls to survive.
But certainly not me,
A young woman of twenty-five.

My Scarlet Letter

Amidst it all, I tried to get onto the dating scene. I had a relationship in graduate school that ended right after my parents split. With all that our family was going through in the process, I longed for something that would make me feel good and forget the pain and stress of it all. So I put a profile on Match.com and winked and chatted with several guys. Having little self-confidence, I was tentative to actually go on dates. In moments of spontaneity, or what I affectionately call "Fuck-it" moments, I ended up meeting a handful of them. Before I looked like a complete bag of bones, I could pass for an alright-looking girl; so a few guys were really interested in getting to know me. One I met and quickly dismissed as he worked where my father did and had the personality of a hairball. Another, we made quite a comical pair because he was a giant, about six-foot-three, and I was not. I had to stand up on a rock when we met for ice cream and mini-golf. At this point, I was not eating much, so I watched him eat ice cream and we actually had fun talking. He would call me when he was at work and we'd chat at night. He invited me to a friend's party, but I was so overwhelmingly nervous about it, that I chickened out. He would tell me how he mentioned "meeting a cute girl from Lynn" to his parents and I freaked. I could not get myself there yet. I wanted to get on the same level, but I was too

My Scarlet Letter

preoccupied with the eating issues taking over my life. Sadly, that connection slipped away because of my lack of effort.

As I was finishing up with grad school, I met up with another person from the site after emailing for a few weeks. We had a lot in common and, though he did not have the accent I love so much, his family was from England. I was going into Boston for a study group to work on a project for one of my classes and he wanted to meet up afterwards and go out to lunch. So I decided to meet in a public place, being the overly responsible girl I am, and give it a go. So I arrived at the Dunkin' Donuts, the meeting spot, just as he called to say he decided to drive in from Quincy and not take the T. So he was driving around the block looking at me standing there like a fool. As I recall, it was misty and he was going to go park in the garage and we'd walk over to P.F. Chang's. He was very polite and we enjoyed each other's company so much we ended up going to a movie afterwards. I went back to the garage with him and he offered to drive me to the station where I parked so I didn't have to take the T by myself. At this point, I felt that he was not a psycho killer and accepted the ride. He was so nervous in the car, he was sweating, but he opened the car door for me, which was sweet. When he dropped me off, he leaned in for the kiss, and I was not expecting it at all. But overall, it was enjoyable yet I never setup another date and distanced myself, yet again. I do not know why I keep doing this when all I want is a mutual love like I see so many others around me experience day after day.

My Scarlet Letter

So I get another wink from a man with a decent profile. Of course, you have to assume that not all of what people type is the truth. But again, we talked online and had a few things in common. He was into music and played bass and I was a visual artist. We had conversations about family and the importance of small things and, when the question of meeting each other came up, I was reluctant to agree, once again. I always think I am going to be a huge let down when I meet these guys and they will be incredibly disappointed. But he is persistent, and I agree to meet. Then, the day of the meeting, I call and get out of it. So we make another date. This time, I went and we met at the mall and went to The Rainforest Cafe. He was tall, thin and resembled Chris Daughtry or a less muscular Vin Diesel. His nose was pierced and he was about eight years older than me, though did not look it at all. I was more nervous than he, but we had fun and he wanted to meet again. But, for whatever reason, I felt that he was more pumped about us than I was. In general, I am terrible at knowing whether or not I truly am into someone, or just enjoy his company. I do not trust many people nor do I trust that I will know "the one" when he comes along. I fear I will be blinded or not paying attention to the right person.

Regardless, we say we will keep in touch and hang out again. At this point, I was not quite so gaunt-looking, so I did not feel completely hideous, just unattractive. As life would dictate, he ended up going away each summer to California. So I did not have to confront my emotions and

My Scarlet Letter

had time to see if I liked him enough to go out again. After returning from his trip, he was ill and had some family issues happening, so I had even more time. Eventually, we made plans after he apologized for his absence. He and I met for a movie, but I made up an excuse about driving my sister somewhere because I was nervous I was going to have to eat something in front of him, because by now, I was ear-deep in my disease. He was kind about it, but I am sure he thought I was crazy and he distanced himself because he thought I was not interested.

Feeling completely confused and frustrated with myself, I sent a message to the second guy I had met and explained how busy I was and apologized for not being in touch. He was not seeing anyone and we talked more online and, gasp, on the phone. (I am not a phone person...at all). We talked late at night and had seamless conversations, usually ending with a question of what I was doing and inviting me various places. Panic, again, set inside my body and I avoided nailing down a day or time. Weeks went by and he was still talking to me. One morning I woke up and thought, "Hey, if this guy hasn't gotten disgusted with my antics by now, I owe him a second date."

That did it. We arranged to meet for coffee at Barnes & Noble's cafe. I remembered what he looked like and had no problem finding him, yet I was a bit thinner and bundled up in layers. Sitting on the table was a box wrapped in tissue paper that, he said, was for me. How sweet is that? Upon tearing the tissue paper off, I saw a little, green satin jewelry

My Scarlet Letter

box. My mind was racing and I couldn't help but to smile as I pondered the significance and thanked him for thinking of me. His response:

"You're welcome, but it is not just a box. I put something inside that made me think of you."

"Oh? Well, now you have peaked my curiosity. You didn't have to get me anything. I wish I had something for you."

"Just open it and you'll see. You'll get it." he said.

Inside the box, was a gift few would understand. He had wrapped up a dozen colored pencils and tied a ribbon around them. Instantly, I thought of a movie each of us enjoyed and quoted in our emails. In You've Got Mail, Tom Hanks and Meg Ryan both love the autumn season and he tells her that, if he knew her address, he would send her a bouquet of freshly sharpened pencils (since fall is back-to-school). So, as coincidences will happen, this guy, Tom, gave me a bouquet of sharpened colored pencils because he knew I was an artist...yea.... I was probably blushing at this point.

So, we had fun, and made plans to go out again, this time sooner rather than later. We decided to have movie night at his place. I felt comfortable enough to agree and, actually went to his place with my Dangermouse DVDs in tow. He rented Count Duckula and had a bottle of wine for us. How on earth could I screw this up? There we are snuggled on the couch, me in all my layers with barely a sip of wine in me, and I fall asleep. We were talking and having fun, then zzzzzz. I was so embarrassed. He let me sleep and then, when I realized what a goof I was, he encouraged me to

My Scarlet Letter

go home and get some sleep and we would do it again another time. I could not believe how I managed to screw things up continually.

What seemed like a good beginning, stalled and never moved forward. I was too ashamed to see him again. I was overly aware of the loss of the pads in my cheeks and my inability to be comfortable.... anywhere. So yet another break with men was upon me. I kept browsing and emailing, not realizing just how destructive anorexia had been to every aspect of my life. I assumed, I would be able to fake normalcy with guys, as I had been doing with other areas of daily life. I watched the television show, Intervention, and saw people in dire straits go off to a center to get fixed. But many of these women had started this disease by age sixteen and have been dancing with the demons into adulthood. Some even had children, boyfriends or husbands. Of course, none of these relationships were healthy, but they had people who cared about them enough to seek help on this show. The ones who were profiled on this show, agree to be filmed for a documentary, no knowing an intervention was coming. Again, I drew parallels and diversions from the experiences that were documented and began to play out my own episode of this show.

Disclaimer: The following program contains subject matter that may be disturbing to some viewers. Viewer discretion is advised. Cue the anxiety-inducing rapid bell music as images of me flash on screen. A clip of my mother

My Scarlet Letter

crying..."She was such a hard-worker and a good kid...I don't know what happened.'

The words: "The Honor Roll Student" pop up on screen.

Next, my brother: "Jen was always a great sister. But now, she is different. This is not the Jen I grew up with." (Tense bells still playing.)

The words: "The Great Sister and the Good Daughter" flash next.

Then, my sister's words: "She looks in the trash to see if we have eaten. She thinks we lie to her, so she makes sure the trash is there. Then she will ask me at least seven times a day, what did you eat? And she freaks out if I do not give her details. It is so annoying."

The description: "The Perfectionist" is read on the televi

Finally, the camera is on me and I stare at the camera explaining what I think is happening to me. I'd say something like, "I cannot eat at the kitchen table.... or in front of anyone for that matter. It was not always like this... I feel every eye burning my skin and feel as if an elephant is standing on my chest. It is so embarrassing." On the black screen, in white letters, the text would read:

Jen is twenty- five and has been suffering from anorexia nervosa for about three years. (Fade...new text) She has agreed to be filmed for a documentary about adult women with eating disorders(fade...new text) She does not know she will soon face an intervention.

My Scarlet Letter

Now the dramatic music continues to play while a preview of the intervention participants and mediator rolls.

On screen, it reads: "Addiction is a disease. (Pause) Most need help to stop. (Pause) This is Jen's story."

In big bold letters, "Intervention" comes up.

Now is when the profiles of each of my family members would roll and video of their daily lives and mine would follow.

I could only imagine the terrible things they would say about me, coming from a place of love and concern. But, sadly, I know not one friend would be profiled because they have all run away. Each one has distanced themselves in his/her own way. No one knew what to do or what to say to me, so they stopped calling and I felt like I had never had any true friends. I know, as a child, I had best friends and throughout college I had some really good friends, too. But as soon as I took a turn down an uncharted path, they vanished. I was always the one people came to with problems and, when a problem took hold of me, I never reached out and no one reached in. It was just about as depressing a situation as I could imagine. My family had to care because they saw me everyday and I was their own flesh and blood. But outside of my immediate family, it was if not a soul had any love for me. I felt I was forgotten and the pain was incredible.

No profile would exist, either, for my father as he would never think of participating in any intervention. He never addressed nor even expressed concern to me about my health, and, was in need of an intervention himself. He

My Scarlet Letter

would assume the tables would turn and he would have to confront his own issues. He found comfort in his own denial and continues to hold onto it to this day.

After showing pictures of me as a child, growing up and graduating, the program would flash to images of me in my bizarre routines and avoidance of social interactions and gatherings. It would show me lose my composure when I could not sit in my usual corner of the couch and cover my knees with blankets, creating a fort where no one could watch me eat a bowl of frozen yogurt. The pictures of my downward spiral (see following pages) would chronicle a sad existence and a loss of the life spark inside.

My mother would sob, frantically trying to blot the tears on her cheeks. My brother would shrug his shoulders and my sister would roll her eyes as she shakes her head in disbelief. I would not be blindsided by the intervention, because I would expect it. They sat me down in the first year of my disease and voiced their concerns, which I found preposterous, at the time. We watched this show together until I began getting chest pains when it hit too close to home, and I had to remove myself from the family room.

So, in my episode, I would show up to the intervention knowing exactly what to expect and feeling powerless over my demons. My mother would have a scripted, emotional letter to read to me. But, I know, they would save her for last and begin with my brother's plea. Then move to my sister's writings, which would undoubtedly shrink my already fragile heart with her sharp tongue.

My Scarlet Letter

    Depending on when the intervention happened, I may not have gone. It was not until I moved passed my denial and started seeking help on my own, that I could even mutter the sentence, "I have anorexia nervosa." Even then, being committed for a last resort. I wrote a letter to my mother, which we both signed, saying I would agree to get treatment if I was not better by a certain date. That date arrived, but I was actively seeking help and seeing my psychologist.

    My fear, for this hypothetical episode, would be that I would agree to go away to treatment and not achieve recovery. I would go and do what I could do, gain ten pounds and return to my self-destructive ways. They would cue the song, Five Steps, by The Davenports and you would see everyone happy and smiling as the update popped up on the screen.

    "Jen spent thirty days at Sunny Horizons and gained eleven pounds. Her family was thrilled. Upon returning home, she lost five of those pounds and is still not consuming enough calories. She is trying very hard, but each day is a struggle.... her family remains hopeful that Jen will make steady progress toward health and happiness."

    Fade to black....

My Scarlet Letter

4
Anachronism

    The thermometer in my car is reading one hundred degrees and the marquis at the bank read a temperature of about ninety-seven degrees. Here I sit in my layers- my thermal pants, shirt, jeans, two light long sleeve tops and my fleece L.L.Bean jacket. On my feet, no flip-flops. Instead, I have sneakers with two pairs of socks. The air conditioner is off, the windows are rolled up and I do not have a drop of sweat on my brow. However, my heated seat is off for a change. How is this possible? It is certainly unhealthy, but so am I. For the past two years, layers have been my existence no matter the season. My arms and legs have not felt the warmth of the sun or the touch of a cool breeze. Simply putting on a t-shirt would send shivers all over my body and, as my Reynaud's Disease kicks in, my fingers and toes would turn purple, then white and feel like they were hit with a sledgehammer. My muscles were weak and, soon, nonexistent. Every day it would get harder and harder to lift objects that never caused me any trouble before. But, now, at the grocery store, I would have my gloves on in the freezer section and I struggled to lift a case of water. How sad that this was what my life had become. But the layers also help to make me look fuller and less frail, but who am I really fooling? I also stopped drinking water. It is weird, but I do not feel I need it.

My Scarlet Letter

Quench
© 2007

Sip & refill-
So frigid
As it coats my throat,
Almost paralyzing,
Numbing.

Glass to mouth-
Moisten my lips
& That's enough.
No need to taste,
Just hold.

Swallow & gulp
Inside my mouth.
No glass....
No sip....
No thirst...

My Scarlet Letter

    I am an unusual case, not only for my age. Today, my therapist called me "atypical" because my onset was not "textbook" as most cases present. It did not start as a diet gone terribly wrong and I did not think beauty lay in my size 00 pants. According to my therapist, other women will keep their "anorexic clothes" and romanticize about the days they fit into them. This is why most suffering goes on for decades. The behavior of women who started as teens and continue into adulthood believe this is typical behavior. Consequently, everyone around them has accepted it as such. So why bother to recover? The existence is enough for these individuals and the aspirations and dreams are nonexistent. They are content with the control and do not desire any more for their lives. After all, if you are skinny then what else is there? You have figured out what most only dream to look like, right? Well, not in my case. I was never proud of how I looked. I felt I could not suffer in silence as pass anything off as normal because I was a different case. Family and friends knew me before the disease and know what it did to me. So, therefore, my actions were unacceptable and bizarre. I was this alien operating under the guise of the person they once knew. I felt like a walking conundrum. I was not what anyone expected and no one could plan how to act around me because I was so volatile. I struggled every minute or everyday with how to make things easy for everyone around me. Most days, I tried to stay out of the way. This meant not sitting at the dinner table or even on the couch with other people. I avoided social gatherings altogether. Sadly, this

My Scarlet Letter

meant missing a close friend's wedding reception. I could not risk drawing attention to myself and away from the bride. I would feel like an eyesore, ruining any pictures including me in them. My sister graduated from high school in 2007 and I did not want to be in her prom pictures because I was a disaster. I was bundled up with layers and she was in a gorgeous red dress. What a memory for her to have to look back on.

I became obsessive-compulsive, as my routine rigidity got so severe. At night, I would only sit on one spot on the couch. If someone sat there, that was it. I would just not sit down at all. When having a bowl of ice cream, I would sit with my knees up and drape a blanket over my legs with the bowl resting in the middle. Then I would stack two pillows to my right so that my mother, sitting in the corner of the sectional, could not see me eat. If my sister came down the stairs and stood behind the couch, I stopped eating. I knew how ridiculous it was and would tell my family, "I don't know why it matters so much where I sit, but I get such anxiety if I cannot be there." I felt everyone watched what I ate, judging why I was eating, what I was eating and how much I was eating. Every morsel was covered in spikes as I swallowed. Sometimes I felt like choking. My mind is so distorted that I feel like a Dali painting. I stick out like a sore thumb and cannot enjoy anything. The control over every miniscule thing in my daily life was completely wreaking havoc on any shred of normalcy I held on to. As I write, I am thinking about my sister waking up and whether or not she will skip

My Scarlet Letter

breakfast or whether she will lie to me? She cannot see the real me and despises interacting with me. It hurts and I know me habits annoy her to no end. This is the clutter that is my brain. How can I focus on anything good? I shiver while showering and fear the cold will send me into shock and I will fall to the floor. And when I wash my hair, I feel like a baby chicken. It is so thin and it keeps falling out. I want to get highlights but I would be embarrassed to go to the salon that has known me since childhood. I have a spa gift certificate that I cannot use because I have no tissue to massage. Pathetic, right?
I would need to gain twenty pounds in the right places in order to pass for healthy and to no look like I am in a competition to be the thinnest. I don't want to eat more than others, but I cannot make myself eat at least the same amount of this health-conscious world. But I can touch my thumb and middle finger together as I put my hand around my triceps. That is wrong. My shoulder blades are like daggers protruding on my back and I have parts of my arms and hips that concave toward the bones. I hate touching any part of my body because it disgusts me. Even the fat pads in my cheeks have disappeared.

    As the list of terrible consequences increases, it makes it harder for me to think I can turn it around at all. My nutritionist tells me that essential fatty acid deficiency is a danger that can be irreversible. Skin stops repairing and loses elasticity. Your hair dries and thins (check that one off already) and your brain starts depleting and makes you

My Scarlet Letter

forgetful and unbalanced. I have so much against me and I cannot see me healthy and balanced. I fear I will blow up like a balloon and be obese because or all of the trauma my body has suffered. It will not know how to process food correctly and I can never again have any normal body functions return properly. I have medicine now to get rid of thrush in my mouth. This thick coating on the tongue is something my grandmother had problems with when she had a blockage in her bile duct. And here I am dealing with it. It is disgusting. I walk slowly and hunch as my bone strength decreases. My ankles swell like an old woman and I cannot lift my legs into my CR-V without my arm's assistance. It is pathetic. You know how those body builders at the gym have veins that stick out? Well, when I look at the top of my hand, it is as if worms and snakes are under my skin. My veins snake and twist like a ribbon dancing in the wind. It frightens me.

    Still, I found ways to make things even worse for my body. I got into drinking maybe three cups of tea throughout the day. Occasionally, I just made the tea to hold the warm cup in my hands. In the days where I did not think it could get any worse, I added a new twist to my disease. I became a thirst anorexic. I began to deprive myself of liquids, not just food. I would not even take a sip of water. When swallowing a pill, I would work up enough saliva to get it down. My nutritionist informed me that this was a new avenue of restriction and that I would, most likely, pass out. Did that stop me? No. Of course, at this point, I was not being honest

My Scarlet Letter

with my nutritionist anyways. She knew though. She would tell me that I smelled of ketones, and this happened when my liver produced glucose in excess and it came out through my skin. I know there is a more technical explanation, but basically she said alcoholics and diabetics sometimes get that faint scent, only detectable to the trained nasal passages. But I still did not care. I would press a water bottle to my lips for show, never quenching my body's thirst. But, in reality, I began to not have a thirst. I had no desire for food or water and no desire to do anything but make it through the day. Every morning I woke up, I was surprised. I figured that with my body eating itself, it would forget to breath overnight (as I felt I forced breaths during the day). My mother would tell me that she would open the door to my room to make sure I was breathing.

Back when my mother was working, she travelled to New York and New Jersey quite a bit. In these days when I was a ticking time bomb, she would be nervous for me, but knew there were other people in the house watching me like a hawk. But one morning, I heard my cell phone ring and picked it up too late. It rang again and saw it was "Mom's cell" so, this time, I grabbed it. On the other end of the phone, I heard "Jen? Where are you? What are you doing? Are you ok?"

"Yes, I'm alright. Why?"

"You are supposed to be at work. Your school secretary called and said you didn't show up and didn't call and no one answered at home so she called me to see if you were ok."

My Scarlet Letter

Holy shit! It was 8:30 and I was still in bed. I heard no alarm or anything. Damn.
"Oh no! Sorry, I didn't hear any alarm or phone. I will call school and tell them I am on my way."
"Jen, I felt so helpless when she called because I am away on business. They thought you got into an accident or something. Are you really awake? Are you up? Don't lay back down."
"Yes, mom. I'm good. No worries." was my calm response. I could tell she was startled and I was just embarrassed to go into work after oversleeping. I felt like an idiot. Again, attention drawn to me in a negative way. I continue to loathe the feeling.

Every conversation is false to me. No one understands what is happening. Every word to me has been said before and they fall shallow. Everyone knows I need help, but nobody helps. They "hope everything is ok" and "let me know if you need anything" as if I am just going to knock or your door and say, "Hey, hi, yea you want to help me out with this anorexia nervosa thing? Awesome, thanks." Are you kidding me? I was this zombie walking around among the living. Any moment, Haley Joel Osment would appear out of nowhere, pointing at me saying, "I see dead people."

It was as if I was trapped in a glass house and everyone saw me suffering. But I wasn't throwing any stones, so why should they? My mother threw stones and made cracks, but I had to be the one to press through those

My Scarlet Letter

cracks and create an air hole for survival. Looking down at my hands, I sustained a lot of damage from that pressing. I wish more people threw stones with intent and force. The few who tap-danced around the issue, threw cotton balls. Those who made a declarative statement to me threw rubber bouncy balls. Depending on the day, my mother threw any ball she could get her hands on. I feel that she tried the hardest, but reached the end of her rope. I had to find inner strength to continue the fight that I only committed to after three years of daily anxiety, desperation and fear. And, to top it off, I was atypical. I was not a teenager who thought I looked beautiful as a skeleton. I was not a model trying to compete in a world of stick figures. I was not even a girl who went on an extreme diet or over-exercised to burn off any trace of a calorie. I was an adult finishing a master's degree and starting a new teaching job.

  To suffer as an adult leaves many more challenges. Had I been under eighteen, I would have been hospitalized without question. But, since I was an adult, I chose not to do that. To go to an inpatient facility would equate to failure for me. This had to be done on my terms or I would never recover. According to the National Eating Disorders Association, anorexia has one of the highest mortality rates of all mental disorders. The average age of onset of anorexia nervosa is 17 years. However, over the past forty years, the number of cases in young women has tripled, whereas teenage onset has remained the same. With this growing demographic of suffering women, I thought it would be easy

My Scarlet Letter

to find help once I was ready. When something is so prevalent as to be plastered on the covers of magazines and affect so many girls and women, I was sure their had to be a network out there for people like me who are fed up with this loss of life. I am an artist and I still have so much I want to do. I still need to get my big break and have my illustrations in books and on magazine covers. And I know in order for this to happen, I have to work on being better to myself

  I was now out of the denial stage and ready to get better. I was only 25 and certainly not ready for my story to end here. I researched local associations and read several books, both personal accounts and more psychological theories as to how this disorder materializes. Nothing quite fit my unique situation, but I kept looking for help and was less than thrilled with my findings. Most treatments centered on teenagers, but would welcome adults. How, though, could I recover in a room full of girls who have totally different perspectives on themselves and life than I do. Adult groups were a great idea and nowhere to be found. The few I came across turned out to be non-existent. All I wanted was help easing into recovery, maybe a couple of hours a week. Even professionals in the field were at a loss for recommendations and agreed there needed to be more resources for women in my situation. Should I have gotten into an in patient program? I would probably feel like I was further along than I am, but hurting in the wallet and priority is given to the young teenage girls. Can you imagine being in your twenties and having to try and recover with

My Scarlet Letter

teenagers? That would not help at all. We would be on a different chapter completely. Not to mention, the art therapy of collaging magazine pictures of models and words would be useless to my recovery and me. Conversations with these young adolescents would make me feel worse.

I sought out a local association, which had a promising lead in their brochure. They had a support group a couple of nights a week and I thought maybe this was just what I needed. In order to get more information, I had to be evaluated be a clinician. This meeting was about a half hour of embarrassing questions as the interviewer wrote feverishly in our moments of awkward silence. After all was said and done, I was told that the support group for women with eating disorders was not the right place for me. How can that be? A woman with an eating disorder does not qualify for the eating disorder support group. I was appalled! Here I went through all of that for nothing. I was labeled too "visibly anorexic" for the group. It is like an alcoholic going to an AA meeting and being turned away because he drinks too much. So who then, I wonder, is privileged enough to receive help? Anyone who has suffered like I have knows just how hard it is to realize that you need help. And here I was pushing open these doors with my deteriorating muscle mass and getting it slammed in my face. I was basically on my deathbed and the easiest thing to do with me, was to commit me. This was not a good enough solution.

My mother has been there every step of the way, from intervening early on, to trying to set me up with a team of

My Scarlet Letter

professionals to help. Had she not done this, I would not be in recovery. I am fortunate that she was there, but what about adults without parents or close loved ones? This disease destroys your life and poisons every relationship you have. When friends and even family members turn away from you, you should be able to get support from somewhere. Without health insurance, I would still be in a very precarious situation. But even with insurance, I had to find someone who would take it. All of the eating disorder specialists did not take my insurance. So, basically, if I wanted a chance at life, I had to spend money from my own pocket. What a predicament to be in. Choose life and go without extra money or keep looking and hope that death does not find you in the meantime.

What did I do? I saw my funeral in a dream. Most of my dreams (pre-disease) were rather alarming and unsettling. One dream I had about my grandfather's death actually came true the morning after seeing it happen. Sounds insane, right? True to form, my funeral dream was no less jarring. In waking hours, I started thinking about a reunion of who came to my graduation party and how they would all fell like they had just seen each other. Everyone would go around saying "What a shame!" and "She had so much promise". They would all think of how I wasted a precious gift and how I was lucky to have what I did, but I got selfish and let it all slip away. I got more and more depressed. I felt this was my destiny, no matter what I did. Whatever I was before, I would never get back and would

My Scarlet Letter

always be branded by this disease. So what's the point? It was a terrible way to feel when you add on my fear that people were mad at me, too. Either they would not show up to my funeral or they would come and be disgusted by me. My great uncle was notorious for being a jerk to his family. He searched through my mother's closets when we first built my home, when I was a kid. At my graduation party, he got in my face asking me if this was because of the divorce and my father leaving. He also fished for information about us seeing my father and wondering why we don't visit him or take care of him. See, meanwhile I was sick, my father had many health issues on his plate. He had kidney cancer and was adjusting to the withdrawals of alcohol and still smoking like a chimney. His skin was grey, his gaze was vacant and he looked about seventy-five years old at times. So I guess he thought I was following in his footsteps. But I wanted nothing to do with those horrible comparisons. How near-sighted was that assumption?

So, as I closed my eyes one night, it was as if I was watching a made-for-TV special of Charles Dickens' A Christmas Carol, minus the ghost of Christmas past. This orchestrated ride of life was going on around me and I felt like I could not get on board. I was standing in line and everyone was passing me by as if I did not exist. I took up no space, yet generated a presence that others made a point to avoid.

My Scarlet Letter

I began to want to live just to spite everyone. They wrote me off as a lost cause and I was about to let them have their moment of glory. Plus, I had no legacy to leave. I was not Elvis or Michael Jackson who died and left a significant, lasting imprint on people's lives. I was an insignificant nobody. Only my immediate family would ever miss the Jen they once knew. I started to think, "This cannot be my destiny. This cannot be the plan." And, if it was, I wanted to prove that I was powerful enough to stop it and reverse it. Could I really turn it around? My plot was dug and my headstone engraved. But I would silence the eulogy. I would make their jaws drop and their heads spin. And before they know what hit them, they would hear my story. They would know what it was like to live with this disease. No one tells the truth in the media. No Michael J. Fox is stepping up for the anorexic and bulimic individuals. No Lance Armstrong brings strength, courage and compassion to the eating disorders. I had to contribute to cracking the taboo.

My Scarlet Letter

5
Anorexic

Cancer is a terrible disease affecting many individuals worldwide. It is rare to find someone that the disease has not affected, be it personally or in the family. No one wants cancer. It chooses them. So this disease is acceptable to talk about because it is so commonplace and we all suffer together. Celebrities have it and there are commercials for medications and treatments. We even have walk-a-thons and fundraisers to bring awareness and, hopefully, a cure. In the card store now there is even a section devoted to cards for cancer patients at each stage of the process- chemo, radiation and hair loss. I think this is a great step forward, and really speaks to those who are suffering

I suffer, not from cancer, but from a disease that does not get any such support except to be misrepresented in the media. If I were to mention Peter Jennings or Patrick Swayze, cancer would not be the first thing you think of. But if I mention Mary Kate and Ashley Olsen, Nicole Ritchie, or Angelina Jolie I don't even need to say the name of the disease because these women are plastered on magazines and are always accused of not eating. It is not something that people setup a benefit for, because it is viewed as a disease of choice rather than one that is genetic. The silly girls/women afflicted with anorexia choose to restrict and, therefore,

My Scarlet Letter

bring the health issues upon themselves. Whereas Parkinson's, Alzheimer's and any form of cancer happens inside the body without the individual selecting it. They are all different diseases, respectively and individually. But there is not a hell of a lot out there in terms of anorexia beyond the celebrities' quests to be eternally thin.

    Well I am here to tell you that I did not choose to have anorexia nervosa. I did not just decide to stop eating to be thin. I have always been a chubby girl and would not look pretty with just skin on these wider-framed bones. It happened all of the sudden, much like any disease does. My symptoms were clear to my family but not to me. I saw them as facts of my existence and not symptoms of sickness. But I was becoming more withdrawn, and I figured it is because I felt I was bringing everyone down by my presence. I was not eating a lot, but I was eating. I was busy in my first year teaching and simply didn't sit down for lunch everyday. Sure, I snacked on something here and there, but I stopped going up to the staff room to eat. So I started losing weight and, boy, everyone thought I was so much more attractive. Even when I lost too much weight and clearly looked ill, people still said how good I looked. Why? Well no one knows what else to say really.

My Scarlet Letter

Witness
© 2006

The rug is thin,
No longer soft,
Bruised and scarred,
With embers of fury.
It wants nothing more
Than to make noise;
To shriek, to tap,
To hum, to whisper
Only silence...
No wonder,
For the frozen cycle
Shall never cease.

My Scarlet Letter

When you have cancer, family and friends flock to your side and hold your hand through the pain. But when you are anorexic, most people who you thought cared about you run the other way. My immediate family, namely my mother was the one who stuck with me most of the time. It was hard for my brother and sister, who mainly avoided me because they were so perplexed by my existence. Deep down I know they care, but they didn't even want to hug me until I told them to. To this day, I feel like I ruined my sister's prom pictures with my layered-up body. Though she will never admit to it. My father, socially awkward on his own, still never acknowledged that I had any issue at all. He would only ask how I was feeling. That became the common phrase right after "How's the car running?" He and my mother divorced in 2005, so my interactions with him are few and far between. My friends were not calling me much and I was surprised. After talking with my older cousin, I started to question whether or not my friends were really my friends. My cousin had a friend when she was younger who was anorexic. She and her group of friends confronted her and went to her parents with concern. Sadly, the girl was still in denial and angry with the friends but they didn't give up on her. I wish I could say anyone outside of my immediate family tried to do anything. I felt written off. It was as if I

My Scarlet Letter

had dropped off the face of the planet or worse, I had fallen beneath the surface.

Even now, as I am in recovery, I still wonder who is there for me. I will do anything for the people I care about. But I still have to remind others and drop hints about things that might brighten my day. Usually, I just keep my mouth shut because I feel that someone should want to do those things and not be forced. It is a dream of mine, to find a person to care about me and love me unconditionally. Instead of me being the one to think about how I can improve everyone else's day, it would be nice to be in the company of someone who did that for me. Even my experiences with online dating confirmed that I never seem to be at the same place as most guys. Though, I did meet a couple of guys who, had I been healthier, I would have continued to date at least a few more times. But I got scared that they would find out about my disease and quickly shied away from them. A mistake, perhaps, but what could I do at that point? Now, I am in a more stable place and would welcome positive energy and love from a man who made me feel special. I would probably have a heart attack from shock if the right man for me showed up and filled my heart with pure love. As I over-analyze everything, I do people-watch and find myself envious of simple, thoughtful, uninhibited interactions with lovers or friends. Most people I meet are so fortunate and will never realize it. For some of us, the very fact that we are alive and breathing is our luck.

My Scarlet Letter

    I used to be of the crowd who would say something like "Eat a cookie!" to the Olsen twins of the world as seen on magazine covers. But now I would never think that because I know just how pervasive and destructive this disease is to those who are honestly suffering. No illness is enjoyable. But there is help for all of it. Even when there seems to be no hope, there is hospice. Meanwhile, I could not even find a support group without being admitted to the hospital. I could not afford to leave work and do that. But I wanted to get a team of professionals as well as be able to talk to those who were in my position. But what I found out was that no one was really in the same place as me, and, most were teenagers. I was warned not to be around "other anorexics" because usually it sparks competition on who can be the thinnest. I did not care to get wrapped up in any of that, all I wanted was to find a balance between health and happiness. And my tank was reading empty on both.

    And I am not diminishing what cancer patients (or any patients) go through at all. I have many people close to me with a variety of ailments. My mother has sent "feel good" baskets to friends suffering with breast cancer and going through radiation and chemotherapy. But what would you send an anorexic? Cookies, cakes and pies? Of course not. It is not all about food. It is about the individual and I could have used anything that would make me feel more like a woman, more like a person, hell, just more alive. I always came last in the order of caring for people, places and things. Just knowing that someone else thought of me enough to put

My Scarlet Letter

me on their radar would have sparked my brain into thinking, "See, you do belong in the equation."

Women with anorexia nervosa are not just depriving themselves of food, some are slowly trying to erase themselves from the world and do not care about the number on the scale. I wish I looked good in clothing and could wear a t-shirt without looking pathetic or freezing and turning white. And do not think for a second that I do not think of the kids I teach seeing me in a fragile state. I never want the girls to look at me and think this is what they need to do. It is quite the opposite. I never want the parents to question my teaching in such a state and not want their children to be in my classroom. This would devastate me because it is my disease and, as I have said, I hate that others are affected by it. It is a very selfish disease and does not discriminate. One cannot suffer with this and not have anyone notice. People notice your body, your movements and your speech. I felt my brain cells dying and felt the words were drifting further from lips and were not there in the right way when I needed them.

Hopefully in a day not too far down the road, we, as friends, mothers, fathers, brothers, sisters, cousins, co-workers and acquaintances we rally around everyone who needs love and compassion. Sadly, I feel those, like me, with anorexia nervosa will not get help without a celebrity putting some money behind the cause. Anorexia and bulimia needs to be addressed just as breast cancer. We need to find a cure for this mental disease. We need to help those who suffer

My Scarlet Letter

younger and younger. In our world of the constant search for eternal beauty, this ideal is not going away. Part of school curriculum should be focused on finding peace inside of yourself. If we don't, the adult life will be plagued with unhappiness and inadequacy. I can tell you, it sucks to be at an age where you should be out enjoying life with friends, settling down and finding your career path. My life was suspended and I went in reverse. Now I have to make up for what was taken away and hope I can turn my life into a positive existence. Imagine if I was able to work out my issues early in life so that the toxicity in my body was eliminated. I feel that it is possible to do this if, as children, we are encouraged to talk about our feelings and understand them. Having someone to talk to outside of the family gives perspective and validity to our thoughts and emotions. I know this sounds contradictory to my opinion earlier stated about psychologists, but my head is on a bit straighter now. Wouldn't it be wonderful if someone made it a mandatory part of a family mental health care plan and every child gets a therapist starting in first grade? Until then, I hope we will freely give handshakes, hugs and smiles. Smiling is free and uses an average of thirteen muscles. So, work those muscles and we, on the other end, will pretend it is not for selfish reasons but, rather, for working toward a morale boost for all.

My Scarlet Letter

6
Agony

Untitled
© 8/15/07

Sound, voice, word-
The over-sensitivities
To insignificance.
Twisting, tightening, throbbing-
The infliction of
Overwhelming emotion.
Clenched teeth, vigilant stare, constant tension-
The inaudible daily
Torment is palpable.
Criticize, analyze, obsess-
A cyclical poison caused
By a parasitic entity.
Reach, persist, believe-
But the trigger
Has been pulled...

My Scarlet Letter

"I cannot stop my mind. I think about what everyone else is doing and create list after list of things for me to do. Kristen and my mother are ready to shoot me because I always ask them what they had for lunch and dinner. Why? I don't know. It puts me at ease for some reason. They ate so I feel like I ate, I guess. They know it is part of my disease, but they still get pissed off. And they know how to give me vague answers that send my head spinning. Here I am worrying about whether or not my sister is going to have a piece of cake tonight. She usually does have some when we have a cake for an occasion but I am convinced she is not going to simply to prove a point to me. Or she will cut a small piece and throw half of it away or something. She is spiting me and I feel like it is intentional hurt. If she goes out tonight and I didn't see her have dinner, I can pretend she is out to eat with her friends or will have a snack or something. But if she is here all night and doesn't have a snack, I will obsess. Grrr... It is so infuriating. I hate that it bothers me to this degree. Hopefully she will tell me what she had for dinner at least. Probably not though. She knows how it affects me.... I am starting to clench my teeth (deep breath, think of something else). Kristen says, "it's feeding the fire" which is true, but it does not make it any easier. Knowing should have no bearing on me, but it does and I am ashamed. If she is out all night, at least I don't have to watch her or wonder when she is in her room intentionally not

My Scarlet Letter

eating or staying away from any room I am in. She waits until I leave the kitchen before she will come in to make anything. It is irritating. I do not want my family working around me and avoiding me. I am like a ghost lurking in the darkness. Even when I am not watching, they think I am.

  This unnatural behavior just makes the environment more uncomfortable for all of us. Hence my earlier comments of things being better in my absence. Don't think I am going to cut myself or tie a rope somewhere, it is just a comment. Yet I cannot help but imagine a better, happier, more productive hone environment for my mother, brother and sister where they don't have to look, listen or interact with me. No more shadow-like presence. They can be normal and not watch me watching everything. I try and stay quiet and inconspicuous to help with that. Ironically, I am conspicuously ill to the eye and cannot help but stand out when I am in public. My mother assures me that my face is looking better day-to-day, but I do not always see it. Why don't I let myself see any positives? Negativity floods my brain and I am constantly on overload. I bought a handheld game to try and distract me. Tetris is great, but it doesn't hit the heart of the issue.

  Damn my madness! Imagine, I am standing here thinking about my mother getting home soon so that she will have a bowl of ice cream tonight. Will she play the "I'm still full" game? She should have plenty of time to digest and I know she is not getting a big meal-salad, chicken or fish. So will I be mad if she opts out of a bowl of frozen yogurt?

My Scarlet Letter

Crossing my fingers that this will not be the case. If she is home by 7, she has an hour to make room. I mean, on weekends she is able to have pizza and a bowl later. Today she only had her cereal and a lunch/dinner combo meal. She does not like cheesecake, so I know she isn't getting dessert at the restaurant. Ooooh...headache why do you assault me? Such tightness. I hope my skull bones stay strong and don't let my teeth fall out and require facial surgery. Damn that book for making me worry about those medical problems. As if I am not already freaked out about dying young and dying like this, in this condition. I think I want to be cremated so the bugs don't feast on me. Pleasant thought, huh? Ok, back to my mother, who just got home and seems to be in a decent mood. It is now 7:30 and she said she shopped after her meal, so I am going to assume that from 6-8:30 is enough time to make room for ice cream, even if it is just a little. Kristen has been napping and will probably go out at some point. If not, I will deal with it. By restricting? No, I have to have more than an Ensure and frozen yogurt. If mom has a bowl, so will I. If not, then an Ensure and maybe something small. I know Ensure is keeping me alive right now, but I don't like them. Nutrients should be from food, not shakes, but I do what I have to do. My worry is that minus the Ensure, I may collapse the next day. So, I have to have it tonight.

  A small positive- I didn't ask Kristen about what she ate last night. That is huge for me (pathetic, I know). Naturally, she didn't notice or acknowledge that kind of

My Scarlet Letter

progress because it is insignificant to her. Oh well. I seem to care more about what she does not do because she seems to offer the least encouragement. So there I go again, gravitating toward the negative. I should focus on mom and Nan's kind words and make better choices. I am so emotionally vulnerable, but I hate showing any of it. I am used to holding it in and keeping it together. But if Kristen doesn't go out and I don't see her eat dinner or a snack, I'm going to go nuts. If she only grabs a handful of grapes and leaves the kitchen, I will not sit for a bowl of ice cream. I don't sit much anyways. Even if mom has some, I will notice the footsteps of my sister on the stairs or the fridge door closing. Or I will check the trash to see if there is any new wrapper or anything in there. My dad moved out and I am the new dark cloud. She hates me right now.

    I keep tricking myself into recovery action and get so proud of little steps of progress. Grasping at the slightest positive is what I have at this point. But when someone diminishes that, the celebration balloon deflates rapidly and the shame roller coaster rolls in. No one has earned this power over me, yet I give it so freely and I should not allow it. Kristen delights in manipulating situations that she knows will set off my obsessive qualities. I hate it and it is the opposite of trying to help me find balance and peace. She is trying to snap me out of it, I suppose. Her going to school gives a healthy distance to this tension. I will miss her but she will be happier to be away from me getting in her business everyday. I hope her heart will still find me. I think

My Scarlet Letter

my family would do better not looking at me. At the same time, my mother would panic about what I was doing when I was not home or not in her sight.

    A perfect example would be my mother's birthday in November of 2007. I love getting unique and thoughtful gifts for my family and friends, so I put a lot of effort into her gift that year. I should mention the Christmas gift I gave to her, my siblings and my Aunt Helen. I gave them indoor skydiving certificates because it was giving them a new, exhilarating experience, or so I thought. A simulated skydive with no danger of plummeting to earth sounded fantastic. But my brother didn't want to do it and my sister still has her gift certificate. But Helen and my mother went with me. I, however, could not participate because of my health. But the two ladies looked absolutely terrified and I assumed they didn't want to hurt my feelings by dropping out. Literally, they both had tears in their eyes after taking the safety class. I pulled them aside and told them this was for fun, not fear. I didn't want them to be upset. But my mother insisted she was going to do it. I am proud to say, they both did it! Helen did not last too long on her first round. My mother felt a sense on accomplishment in doing it. But, if I had it to do again, I would not have spent all of that money on something that was not received in the way I had hoped. I built it up in my mind only to be knocked down with lack of enthusiasm.

    But this time, it would be better. I got my mother tickets to see a Cirque du Soleil show. The big surprise was that it was at Madison Square Garden, so we would be

My Scarlet Letter

traveling from Boston! I bought plane tickets and told her to take the day off of work. As an added bonus, I called up her good friend, Gloria, who worked in Manhattan and had her take the day off to meet us at the show. The kicker was that I got two tickets for them to go to the show and I was just going to go hang out in Times Square for the duration of the performance. It was expensive and I did not want to be a "third wheel" and allow them to catch up and have fun. But, once again, it was too big of an idea. The morning of her birthday, my mother was immediately skeptical because it was a surprise. I just told her get in the car and go with it. When we ended up at the airport, she was truly worried. I gave her the tickets to the show and she was flabbergasted. I was excited for her and, inside, my stomach was in knots about the plane ride. I was not sure how my body would react to the altitude. She could not even show excitement for the gift because this was what was already occupying her mind. Though she did not say it. Lucky for us, she pulled some strings and got us on an earlier flight because she is a frequent flyer on these shuttle flights.

As I buckled myself, I took long, slow breaths and knew there was no turning back. As soon as the rumbling of the wheels at take-off subsided, I felt the pressure in my chest and closed my eyes. My mother tried not to stare directly at me, but I knew she was paying attention. It was like an elephant was standing on my chest, taking a break to scratch his trunk with one foot and then stepping down again. Luckily, it did not last the whole time. But, on a short

My Scarlet Letter

flight, the descend came quickly with more weird feelings. "Please don't pass out. Please keep my heart going. It is my mother's birthday." I repeated this to myself over and over. I also was singing Alanis Morrissette's song, "Ironic" in my head. There is one verse that says,

> "Mr. Play It Safe was afraid to fly
> He packed his suitcase and kissed his kids goodbye
> He waited his whole damn life to take that flight
> And as the plane crashed down he thought
> "Well isn't this nice..."
> And isn't it ironic... don't you think"

I thought back to my first plane ride to Disney World when I was seven years old. We hit turbulence during the flight and I wrote my will on a napkin, convinced we were going down. Since my family was on the plane, I think I left my NKOTB tapes to one of my friends from elementary school.

Thank goodness I made it through that and now, landed safely in New York City. Again, my mother got us a ride from her usual driver at the car service used by her company. Meanwhile, it was about lunchtime and I asked if she was going to eat. She asked me the same thing. So we were going to split a bagel. She had a couple of bites and I waited for her to go to the bathroom before ripping off a piece to stuff in a napkin. It was like this competition and

My Scarlet Letter

she didn't eat three square meals either. Yet, no one was on her case. Everyone was only on mine because I was slightly slimmer and they didn't see me eat because I would not sit down with them. It was so infuriating. But, in any case, she knew I pretended to eat so we could focus on her fun birthday.

Now, remember, it is November so it is chilly and very windy. I am layered, as usual. We got to Madison Square Garden and I texted Gloria, my mother's friend, under the guise of one of my friends. We were early and I had brought a couple of snack bars. We went to a Barnes and Noble and I gave my mother one of the bars and, again, said I ate mine without her seeing it. Of course, she was less than thrilled, but I tried to focus on the show. We went to wait by the entrance and I got nervous about Gloria's arrival. We lingered for a while as my stomach did somersaults. But as I glanced to the left, there she was! My mother said "Oh...my...god" and the two of them were like teenagers giggling and hugging. So I think that part of the surprise was successful. She could not believe I got her to come for the show (they had not seen each other in months).

Now, remember, the kicker was that I was not going to the show. Instantly, my mother's face got longer. "Where are you going? Why didn't you get yourself a ticket? I don't want to leave you here for two hours."

"I'll be fine," I said. "I am heading down to Times Square to meet up with a friend from Lesley. I want you guys to have fun." It was clear my mother was not fine with this

My Scarlet Letter

idea. She saw me struggle to stay upright in the winds while walking down the street. But I was leaving and she was going to the show, she could not stop me. I waved and smiled as they went inside and I am sure she commented about me leaving. I didn't care, I wanted her to have fun with her friend and not think about me.

It was damn cold and the wind did get to me, but I walked from Madison Square Garden to Times Square anyways. I shopped around in stores, not buying anything, of course. I did not really meet anyone, so it was kind of boring after a while. But I walked a lot, making sure not to waste all of my energy for the walk back. My hands were getting purple and I could feel my breath lessen its pace. I got nervous and kept walking toward Madison Square Garden with my head down. The crowds actually helped to block the wind, but I knew I needed a break from it soon. If I did not make it back to the entrance, my mother would freak out. If I had collapsed, I would have been trampled and, probably, robbed of my purse. Well, maybe a nice person would find me and not take my money but, rather, call for help. If I ended up in an ambulance, I knew a hospital stay was inevitable. Then my mother would call my cell, find out and have to stay in New York City because of my fall. But, maybe I could say I am staying with a friend and she can go back home and not have to be inconvenienced.

Then, all of the sudden, I was at the entrance to Cirque Du Soleil and the crowd was exiting. My rampant mind had distracted me enough to get me to my next stop.

My Scarlet Letter

Sad, but my life had become a series of checkpoints. I broke my day down by where I needed to be and when, and would cross off the spot on my list (not believing I actually would get things accomplished). But I could see the relief in my mother's face when she saw me there. I hate that she was worried on her day that I tried so hard to make special.

My Scarlet Letter

Conversation
© 2007

The door is closed
& I hear whispers.
Press against the barrier,
"Oh how I miss her."

The breaths are quick
& I hear the tears.
My throat plummets,
She voices her fears.

The pain is real
& It slows my heart.
I do not understand,
I thought I was smart.

Ear to splintered wood
And it has never ended.
Each minute I wait & hope
Her heart will be mended.

My Scarlet Letter

7
Annihilation

Going Going Gone
© 2009

Always a bottle on the shelf
Going, going, gone...
Though I'd never drink one myself
Going, going, gone...
Every night he'd have them
Going, going, gone...
Every night we'd ask him
Going, going, gone...
We never had a chance, so
Going, going, gone...
Caring less and less, it showed
Going, going, gone...
No laughs, no tears, no smiles
Going, going, gone...
Eggshells around all the while
Going, going, gone...
"Enough is enough!" she said.
Going, going, gone...
"Then I will just leave," he said.
Never told us where or when
Going, going, gone...
Didn't care to see us again?

My Scarlet Letter

Going, going, gone...
Random gifts left at the door
Going, going, gone...
What they hell is this all for?
Going, going, gone...
Two daughters and a loyal son
Going, going, gone...
We always wondered what we had done
Going, going, gone...
The youngest will go far for sure
Going, going, gone...
The oldest has a heart so pure
Going, going, gone...
As for me it's never clear
Going, going, gone...
He almost lost me just last year
Going......
                Going....
                              Gone.....

My Scarlet Letter

So where did it come from? The easiest answer would be my parents' divorce. Yet this may only have been the catalyst. I do not think my father moving out and the actual divorcing from my mother made me anorexic. I never felt close to my father and was not a daddy's girl (in any sense of the word) missing my father/daughter bond. How can you miss something that was never there? If anything, the divorce allowed my mother, brother, sister and I to walk around our house with a lighter heart, no stepping on eggshells. No longer would I hear the garage door open and dread my father's footsteps coming up the cellar stairs.

I am one of three children, sitting in the middle of the sequence. Yet, I also feel I have qualities of both the middle and the oldest child, as far as theories go. I was the first to drive, go away to college and the one my younger sister asked for permission to go to a friend's house when my mother was at work (not my father). My older brother has Asperger's Syndrome and had a lot of struggles growing up. My father, an emotionally unavailable alcoholic, had no compassion or understanding of my brother's issues. To this day, I do not believe he really grasps what autism is. He would often yell at him for speaking too loudly or get mad at any of us for saying "Hi" twice in one day. Being seven years older than my sister, I wanted to protect and interject whenever I could so that she would not soak up the negativity my brother and I got from our father. I do not think it was a feasible task because no matter what I did, he found a way to make us feel

My Scarlet Letter

like crap (for lack of a better word). I remember when my sister went to swim at a neighbor's house and forgot a towel. She came back to the house and my father was there before I was, saw her dripping wet and told her she had to stay outside until she was dry because she did not have a towel. Luckily my brother was there to unlock the door and let her in. I knew I could not do everything I wanted, but I was certainly not going to stop running interference because I wanted to fill that void for my sister and let her know that her brother and sister cared even if she could not feel the love from her father. Apart from him, the four of us, including my mother, had created a supportive family unit.

Like a ghost, my father was there, but not. He spent most of his time in the basement when he was home, having a few glasses of coffee brandy in his den of cigarette smoke. He worked 6 to 3 building jet engines for General Electric. As a child, I always assumed he worked until 5 because this is when we saw him everyday. But everyday after work, he went to the Hibernian's for a drink and to watch sports with the guys. He loved sports and was once a great athlete. My mother made a scrapbook of all of his newspaper clippings, including a caricature done of him. He was a local all-star and almost went professional after play semi-professionally and being scouted by two professional baseball clubs as a teenager. He could have been a Chicago Cub or a New York Yankee, but his story is that he stayed local for my mother(who he was head-over-heels in love with). She told him to go and not miss out on a great opportunity, but he

My Scarlet Letter

knew she was not going to follow. That began a progression, or regression, of a seemingly happy, talented man into a jaded, disgruntled blue-collar father who could never take pleasures in simple joys such as playing with his kids. He always told me how he hated working at his job and kept the cards from the scouts in his wallet. It was as if time was frozen and the one thing he knew how to do and enjoyed, slowly drifted away from his grasp. Perhaps turning to the drink made him forget about what his life could have been. I think this played into a lot of repressed anger he held.

This angered materialized into negativity towards everyone around him, namely his family. The boys at the Hibernian's still liked him because they all grew up together and have a history. But as soon as he came home, it was reality. He was not a Yankee (or a Cub); he was a father and a GE employee. It was not glamorous but, had he embraced it, the love of his wife and kids would have filled him with light and made his days full of life. Instead, a permanent scowl seemed to be on his face. We were doomed to fail in his eyes because we could never please him. No matter how helpful we were or how well we did in school, we always did something to set him off.

Once my father moved out, this dark cloud was lifted, but not gone. We were so used to negativity that someone had to be the default. It turns out it was me. Every time I spoke, I was told I had a tone. Every day I came home from work and didn't smile consistently, I was pissed off. I felt

My Scarlet Letter

like I wasn't in control of my emotions, rather they were being decided for me. My family said I was mad, so I would not be able to change their minds. In reality, being "on" at work teaching 7 classes and 150-175 children takes a lot of effort and energy. By the time I come home, I thought I didn't have to perform and I could just decompress. But my expressions were not animated enough and my family always thought I was on their case or aggravated. How could I compete with five people in my house painting me as a negative person? I was hurt and did not know how to change. I thought they would love me for me. But I started to stay out of the way and not talk as much in an effort to avoid any misconceptions. But I couldn't win and I kept feeling the pit of my stomach grow bigger and sting longer. I let everyone's poor image of me penetrate my thoughts and I started to believe that my presence was detrimental to each of them. I was causing my mother more stress when she was trying to heal from the divorce. My brother and sister were trying to enjoy not having to walk on eggshells around our father's negativity and, for some reason, I unintentionally took that away.

     The focus during this time became a renovation of the house that would involve an in-law apartment for my grandparents. They were going to sell their house and move in with us. The plans drawn up by the architects looked fantastic and we knew we were in for months of inconvenience, but the outcome would be great. My grandmother's health has not been up to par and she had a

My Scarlet Letter

couple of surgeries that significantly impacted her strength and mobility. Ironically, one of her surgeries came about because she went into depression and stopped eating after we noticed her jaundice. She had the Whipple procedure done which rerouted her digestive tract and she made a remarkable recovery. But there were times when we were planning for the worst because she could not even stand up from the recliner. So, my mother decided that this was a great way for them not to worry about the upkeep of a house and give my grandfather some support in her care. They had a great setup planned, including a chairlift on the stairs to the garage so she can get to the car. The bathroom had grab bars by the shower and an elevated toilet seat and a washer and dryer within steps of their recliners.

      This project evolved into a facelift for our house, too. Originally, it was just an addition, but the renovation turned our house into a beautiful residence. The backyard has no more pool, the shed was moved and a new deck was built with two doors to access the house. We added on a sunroom in the back and built a basement bedroom for my brother that turned out to be his bachelor pad. Our kitchen was gutted and we got new appliances, cabinets, granite countertops and an island with a tile floor underneath. It was a far cry from the brick-patterned laminate and the dark cherry cabinets that held so many negative memories. My mother was eradicating the house of my father's imprint. We would no longer see the corner where he prepared his coffee brandy or the cabinet where the bottle was kept. No more

My Scarlet Letter

ashtrays under the sink. This renovation was cathartic for her and this is why she kept going. It became so that every room had something done to it. The dining room had new furniture and two new doors leading to new spaces. Track lighting was everywhere in the downstairs of the house. Upstairs, new carpet and new floors. She got a new mattress and changed the bathroom, adding tile and a new shower. The outside of our house got new vinyl siding and pillars on the front steps. Our driveway was no longer black hot top; instead she had grey pavers installed. The list goes on and she felt better each time something was completed. But it was a long year of living in weird spaces sectioned off by plastic. I still found a way to keep my obsessive tendencies and, when summer came, I was around a lot more while the workers were there. They were good guys, but I found myself going out a lot, returning around lunchtime to make something for my brother and see if mom was coming home to check on the progress or if she was eating with Joe at work. I would make hot tea and run errands. It was a very consuming project for everyone, but by the end, my mother was a new woman. She could actually feel at peace in the house. It was touching to see her so happy and proud of her house.

The finished masterpiece coincided almost exactly with Kristen's high school graduation. So the decision was made to have an open house/graduation party because everyone has been speculating about what the house looked like and making comments about the size of the project. The

My Scarlet Letter

gossip-hungry extended family members where chomping at the bit to get a glimpse. The house was gorgeous and well suited to entertain but, as with my party, it brought trepidation. Would my great uncle look in closets and sneak around again? Would my father show up and be offended? Could I stay out of the way, yet be helpful? I tried, I really did. But everyone noticed that I did not eat. How could I with everyone paying attention to it so much? I mean, at this point, I had not sat down for Christmas, Thanksgiving or Easter dinner at the table. I cleaned the whole time or pretended to take a plate to the living room. So I just continued to walk around and make small talk until everyone was gone. I thought I had gotten through it alright, I guess. Most people had already written me off. My father's side of the family looked into my eyes with disbelief when I said I was fine. I wasn't going to tell them anything because it was the story to spread and not me they cared about. My father naively asked how I was doing or maybe he asked if I was feeling okay. I now know that my godmother and another friend of my mother had cried when seeing me. But my father, true to form, showed no emotion and no interest in my failing condition. The most he did was ask my mother how I was doing.

Some say it is his fault I became anorexic. But my therapist agrees that it would have happened with him in the house. Many young girls with alcoholic or abusive father figures will have eating disorders. But, remember, I was the rock and helped keep up the "happy family" image we four

My Scarlet Letter

worked so hard to convey. So my father contributed to my low self-image, for sure, making jokes and faces when I would have to adjust my glasses by scrunching my nose. But I think with the overall pressure I put on myself that my perfectionist personality and my responsibility to my family and friends were significant factors. I am hyper-vigilant and often absorbed everyone's negative emotions whether I wanted to or not. I would feel guilty if my mother was upset over something and I could not fix it. I would beat myself up for saying something in the wrong way and upsetting my brother. If my sister was pissed off at a friend or had a bad day at work, I felt like I was in the wrong and longed to get her out of a funk. This is not a healthy way to exist. If a friend was having a tough time, I would go home thinking about what I could do to better her situation. In relationships, I was always too thoughtful and it was never reciprocated. I anticipate people's needs so that they can see that I care and I am not self-centered. I am a genuine person who tries hard to please everyone and cannot find the key to happiness for myself. I can only hope that I will, but it feels so out of reach. I feel like I am perpetually on a treadmill, only fooling myself that progress is being made.

  When my father moved out, I was the negativity sponge. Since I show no tears, I suppose everyone thinks I can take it and it does not matter. Perhaps they do not realize they do it because it has become so habitual. No one ever has to worry about Jen because she can handle it all. I guess I thought I was pretty strong and could take whatever

My Scarlet Letter

people threw at me, not knowing the consequences. But if I had an outlet for my anger, it would only be a partial release because my mind still runs a marathon. Don't get me wrong; my art is a crucial release and a tool for me to navigate my existence. But when I am creating for others or not able to do my real work, it does not have the same therapeutic effect. The painting process is a release, but mostly off current issues of the day or week. The repressed emotions stay there, buried. I believe that these emotions sat and festered inside, converting to a poison attached my vital organs, including my brain. This is what almost removed me from this earth. This is what dragged me underground and starved me of sunlight and warmth. This poison has no antidote. It was not annihilated and, it still fights with me each day.

My Scarlet Letter

Absorbent
© 2009

Give it to me,
I'll take it
If it helps.

Don't feel bad
I'll make you laugh,
If it helps.

If you shed tears,
I'll wipe your cheeks.
If it helps.

Feeling down?
I'll give you a hug,
If it helps.

Don't want to be alone?
I'll come over and hang,
If it helps.

Mad at the world,
Yell at me,
If it helps.

My Scarlet Letter

A friend betrays,
But I am here
If it helps.

Can't decide?
I will listen
If it helps.

They walked away
But here I am
If it helps.

Every time
I am here for you
If it helps.

Never about me
I remain for you.
If it helps.

I need someone
But never mind.
If it helps.

Your life is full
I will remind you
If it helps.

Jen Dubis 2010

My Scarlet Letter

My heart is heavy
Yours is light
Hope it helps.

Why do I do this?
It doesn't seem right
Hope it helps.

We all should try
Not just some
If it helps.

How wonderful
To have a true friend.
I know it would help.

But I'll be forgotten
Find someone new
Hope it helps.

My Scarlet Letter

My father never acknowledged my sickness and still does not say anything about it. The poem at the beginning of this chapter is something I wrote when thinking about how disconnected with life he is and how he will never be there for any of us, as he should. I might as well be dead because he does not treat my siblings or me like we are living. We are not an integral part of his life and he does not care to work towards changing that. My brother's high school never knew he had a father until graduation day because they never saw him at any meetings for five years. He would come to Kristen's softball games to stand in the back because his baseball genes were not being wasted. But he was not one to cheer, smile or clap. When he came to pick me up from college in Connecticut, he would stand at the door and ask where my bags were and load up the car. No hugs, no "I miss you", no care really. At my graduation dinner with my roommate's parents, he said nothing. They asked me later if he was alright. I was embarrassed that this was normal behavior for him. He has limited social skills and, it seems, a limited interest in his children's lives. I cannot change this and I have accepted that. It is a disappointment for all of us, but one that only we have grasped. His side of the family still believes we wronged him and we have cut him off entirely. Again, it is sad that they will never see our perspective. They do not know that we are good people who have covered for him and, without us, he still would not have gone to a doctor.

My Scarlet Letter

His life is better because we care about him. How can someone not reciprocate or appreciate?

It seems illogical, but he has never been capable of relating or communicating. Before he left, I confronted him in the basement, which required a significant amount of mental and emotional preparation. Even then, he was non-responsive. I expressed my concern for him leaving and planning on not telling us where he was going. He wanted to fulfill that victim role to the end. Poor him, pushed out of the house by a family that hates him. And here I was trying to build a bridge, trying to reconcile wasted years with compassion. All he could say is, "Well, we've never really had one of those father-daughter relationships." My throat constricted as I muttered, "And how does that make you feel?" The worst possible response was no response at all. He turned away from me as he glanced over his shoulder and partially shrugged. I could not say another word and turned to walk up the stairs feeling like I swallowed a box of nails.

My Scarlet Letter

Paradoxical Existence
© 2005

So far away,
And yet within reach,
As I stretch, it tears
And still I cannot succeed.

Unresponsive
You lie still
As always, never smiling
Ever static and absent.

My voice but echoes
In the hollows-
Fractured and strained
Everyday...further.

Only you, not us-
Victim for life
By choice it seems,
Perpetual isolation

Come back please,
Before it falls.
I fear it is lost,
But still no sound.

My Scarlet Letter

Cynical investigator,
Rambling accusations
Devoid of color
Confusion wins control.

Stop! Try- would you?
The answer remains
Constant negativity
My breath grows heavy.

You tremble, I see.
Caged tears cascade
Met with aggravation.
Never dormant.

Where are you?
Tell me what happened.
I am still here waiting
Grab my hand, if only once...

My Scarlet Letter

    Well, when my father moved out, around the holidays, he did so in a secretive manner. He left with a couple of bags and did not say a word. He gave us each a hug, if that, and was gone by the time we returned from daily routine plans. No forwarding address was left and no real way to communicate if we needed him. As I write this, it sounds even more ridiculous than when it was actually happening. Imagine three caring individuals, who are also your children, offering to help move you in to your new apartment and asking if you need anything. Then imagine you not answering, not looking the least bit upset or remorseful and driving away from them and never looking back.

    Fortunately, I had done some sleuth work and found the name of a property management company on his key ring and looked up the apartment complexes owned by this company in the area. I knew he would not go too far, since he worked in our city. So I narrowed it down to a couple of places and drove around looking for his car. I could not believe I was doing this and, initially, I felt like I was doing something wrong. I thought I should not be hunting and I should let him lead his own life. But, whether he cared or not, I wanted to know where he was going to live. He may not be my mother's husband anymore, but he is still our father... or he should be. After getting lost in some of the parking lots, circling the buildings, I saw his Kia parked near the dumpster. So, I threw my car into park and grabbed the note I had written from my purse and placed it under the wiper blade on his windshield. I needed him to know that it

My Scarlet Letter

upset us that he did not tell us where he was going and for him to know that we still wanted to be in touch.

Unfortunately, he was still mad at my mother and, consequently, me because he thinks I am her clone. So he remained distant and emotionally unavailable. He sunk into depression and his already compromised health declined so much that he needed surgery on his kidney. At this point, I was not at my worst, but he continued to withhold information about his condition, being very cryptic in his phrasing about what was happening. All we knew is that his kidneys were not working well and there was a blockage. He needed surgery and, again, I asked what he needed. His sister was taking him to the hospital, so he said nothing. The day before going in, he dropped off an envelope for me in the mailbox. He had given me his will, naming me the executrix in case something happens. What do you do with that shock? I was completely unprepared. But, we went to visit him in the hospital after the procedure, awkward as it was to be in the room with my aunts. Prior to this procedure, he had a rod put in his ankle and was in the hospital for a day and we did not visit because he didn't seem to want us around. So my aunt still held slight contempt toward us, I think. But this time, surgery saved his kidney and removed the cancerous tumor.

My Scarlet Letter

The Spin
© 2009

I know how it looks,
I know how it seems.

Kicked out before the holiday,
How cruel, how mean.

No one visited,
No one cared.

This lonely soul,
Left in solitude, scared.

Did you know
He never really said goodbye?

Nor did he mention
Where he was going to reside.

He made no effort
And refused help of any kind.

I would constantly wonder
What could be going on in his mind?

Fresh eyes cannot see
The pain from so many years.

These eyes will only assume
We caused all the "tears".

My Scarlet Letter

My father is an enigma of sorts. He was once a popular athlete with friends and a future with a beautiful young woman he would end up marrying. But, as I look back, I do not ever remember him being happy around his own family. He was always mad about something and usually drinking after work. He complained about everything and seemed to "go through the motions" of existing day-to-day.

After living alone, things had not changed. He still remains to be awkward around us and there is never an attempt to truly reconnect. His life was saved that one day on the stairs when he had a small stroke and almost fell backwards. My mother and I pulled him up the stairs as his eyes, glossed over and fixed straight ahead, did not blink and his fingers tensed like claws while his legs bent. Refusing medical care, he was angry with us and, I believe, is still mad today.

Unfortunately for us, when he passes, his family will place blame on his three children for "abandoning" him and "not being there". I can see it play out like a movie complete with dramatic pauses and epic music. They will never understand the real story because they do not have the capacity to do so. After all, you do not want to believe anything negative about someone you care about, especially family.

My Scarlet Letter

8

Altruistic

Change
2009

Change is coming,
Don't be afraid.
Be open. Be excited
Be one who will accept the uncertainty.
Definite possibilities lay at your feet.
Pick them up.
Activate each, one by one.
Watch them move-together at first,
Then finding internal inspiration from the uplifting surge of
energy pulsating around each changeable form.
One is leaning, one is split,
One is staggering and one is broken.
All are evolving.
All are set in motion by action and intent.
 Change is here.
 Embrace and enjoy it.

My Scarlet Letter

Admitting I have a problem was hard enough. Acknowledging that this disease infected me and saying it out loud was another story. It was a gigantic step that I had to make and I know my family supports me. But how long will it take to be free? How long can I last? My body has already withstood more than most bodies can. Will I ever be back to a state that I consider to really be me and only me? If simply plumping up meant recovered then, yes, eating a cookie would be great. But it is not just a physical disease and most will relapse and struggle for decades with the recurrence. I simply do not have time to go in and out of hospitals for treatment and I never want to be admitted into a program. In all reality, the doctors should have kept me long ago. I should not be standing.... the experts agreed.

But for one reason or another, my abnormal body has been able to keep going despite the torturous abuse I have given it. I did not go into cardiac arrest, though, I felt my heart slowly pound through my skin many times. I do not know how I was able to continue working and going about my daily life. There were many days when I was surprised to make it through the day and arrive home safely. Everyone was thinking to himself/herself, "This girl is going to die." and were preparing themselves for it. At work, one of my student's nurses told me she planned out in her head what to do if there was a code at school. She had mapped out how to get to me and who would cover her student. I was shocked that she had thought about it that much. Come to find out, the school nurses had considered the "what ifs" as well. But I

My Scarlet Letter

think a turning point came from an unexpected source. My new principal, who was aware of my disease, brought me into his office to check-in with me. He told me that staff had been expressing concern to him and want to know if I am doing okay. No one wants to ask me directly, for obvious reasons. But then he told me that parents had also expressed concern. One parent had come to him in tears over my condition. My jaw dropped and I felt more embarrassed than normal. This was not going to end well. Parents get upset and then they will want to get rid of me because I am an eyesore and not setting a good example for their children. I was nervous and, in some way, touched that a parent cared enough to shed tears for me. I never thought anyone from my work community truly cared about me. If parents were crying, what were kids thinking?

Once I started to gain weight, I knew what they were thinking. One of my first graders asked if I was pregnant. Nice. That was just what I needed to hear. I felt like a planet already and, if I was pregnant, at least I knew the belly was going away and I would have a precious little baby to distract my worries. But that clearly was not the case. Meanwhile, my worries would always find my sister. I find myself concerned with transference of this disease affecting her. I see her trying to stay a certain size. I see her drinking coffee more than eating and think about how it is acting as a diuretic for her system. I have learned so much about nutrition, thanks to Martha, and I cannot help but go back to what she has told me. She explained what the body needs

My Scarlet Letter

and I know my sister is smart, but she could easily go too far (as any girl could). I hope that seeing me in a desperate condition will remain etched in her mind if she ever feels like skipping meals. She is so beautiful and has a great head on her shoulders, but I still worry. I know she harbors a myriad of feelings toward my father and me, respectively. In my heart, I want her to keep my love in hers. I know that this disease has the power to spread in families, and it is natural to worry. She is tall and thin and does not eat healthy as it is. Her diet is coffee and cigarettes, primarily, and my heart would bleed through my skin if she ever turned down that path.

  As for me, I knew I could not just gain ten pounds and recover. Even if I got to the minimum acceptable BMI, it would be too easy to go back. I would be a decade-long victim if I remained on the blurry line. I had to get past it or I would either die or never recover. For me, this meant doing it on my own, without a program. Honestly, the whole hospital thing turned me off after my experience of being labeled "too visibly anorexic" for a support group. There was no way I was surviving unless I made the commitment to do whatever it takes. I had no idea what was going to happen. All I knew is that every single day that I tried to eat more, I ended up with tears of fear in my eyes and panic in my chest. I would tell others that I was eating more than I really was. But, if I wanted to stay out of the morgue and without a feeding tube inserted, I had to force feed myself.

My Scarlet Letter

    At this time, I was trying out medication to help with my stress and withdrawn behaviors. My body did not like these at all. I started with Lexapro and started to have sleep problems, but did feel a bit less upset. It was not a huge dose, but I did not want to rely on medications for the rest of my life. But I knew I did not have a lot of time left on my watch. I felt like I was going to die without taking a leap. My sister gave me a perfect card with a duckling on a diving board. It was nervously standing on the edge looking down. It was symbolizing me swallowing my fear and diving into recovery, no matter how uncertain and scary it might be. She was showing her support in a subtle and loving way and I really appreciated it.

    I had to be careful of re-feeding syndrome where the body cannot absorb the nutrients, thus preventing weight gain. I know this sounds great, but when your heartbeat and oxygen in your lungs depends on gaining weight, it can be a steel clad death sentence. I made myself think this might happen. Either that or I would become overweight because I lost my metabolism and my ability to effectively function internally. But I did eat and slowly gain. It was a source of stress and, initially, I could only really eat at night, when people were not watching. I ate a little bit more each day and had trouble with sleep. I did not recall getting up and eating, but I went through a box of cereal in one night or a big bag of dried goji berries. This horrified me and was my worst fear about the recovery process materializing. I gained weight from the medication and the night eating and was freakish.

My Scarlet Letter

But the question I had was, when do I stop being considered anorexic? I gained too much weight and certainly did not "look" anorexic, yet some behaviors were definitely still present. I was not eating regularly because of the night eating and, sometimes, it was sleep eating. I did not know I was doing it until I woke up to an empty cereal box. Or worse, my mother would say she heard me awake at night. I was so embarrassed and did not know what to do.
The medicines were not helping me feel my best and joined the local YMCA to see if I could rebuild my muscles. I could not even lift 2 lb weight and do a set of curls with them. I started doing a gentle yoga class and got irritated with myself because I could not relax and focus on my breathing. My mind does not shut off, ever. I am still looking for the off button. The instructor was really sweet and tried to give some tips. My balance was not there and my muscle tone was non-existent. I moved on from Lexapro to Celexa and thought it would help. It was alright, but I still could not sleep through the night.

  I tried to meditate; I tried taking melatonin and putting lavender under my pillow. Nothing really worked. I was given a sample of Lunesta, and did not sleep a wink the night I took it. It seemed hopeless, but I did not give in to taking sleeping pills because I did not want to rely on them for a good night's sleep everyday. I wanted my body to recover without dependency. But because I tried 3 different SSRI's in a matter of months, I think my body got even more out of whack. I try to keep in perspective, because my

My Scarlet Letter

situation is unique. Only time will tell what other damage has happened internally. But I am certainly healthier and have more of my personality back, which is good. But I am still not alright with being good to myself. When I was not being good to me, neither was anyone else. Still, I feel no one is good to me unless bound to me by familial ties. I think I give so much to compensate for the lack I feel. I am worried that I will never find a balance and be alone for whatever life I have left.

Boy, does that sound grim or what? It is an honest admission, though. I am here, but I am not sure what will happen to me now. I know that I avoided a couple of possible matches from blind dates because I did not think I was worthy of a decent person and I was anticipating one of us letting the other one down. I was not even thinking of the many positives that could have come from a new relationship. I started and then let my head get in the way. As previously mentioned, I let someone get close to me before the disease and he really was not mature enough to care about me. I drove an hour to see him on Valentine's Day after student teaching all day. He was in college and I was finishing my Master's Degree program. I was all excited about the gifts I got for him because they had an inside meaning between us. Not only did he not get it, but he gave me a little snoopy from CVS with a little candy heart-shaped box. I was so disappointed, not in my gift, but in the fact that he put no thought into it and did not interpret the significance of my gift. I knew then that he could not make

My Scarlet Letter

me happy for I needed someone who would anticipate my needs before or simultaneously when I was thinking of his. This was how out-of-balance I was. I wanted a man who would be on the same page with me and care about me and be endeared by my quirkiness and I to his. But this quest, I feel, may never end. And at this point in my life, I have resolved to just let life happen and not to have an expectation. I have to focus on myself in a non-selfish manner. I need to restore myself to a place where I can only bring good to others and stop putting the negatives on myself.

     I even reconnected with the Chris Daughtry look-a-like who I had seen twice before. We met at the Cheesecake Factory and I was beyond paranoid that he would be repulsed because I had gained so much weight since he saw me last. It did not seem to bother him, but I was honest with him about not being healthy before (not mentioning an eating disorder) and he said I looked much better this time than before, which was a relief. I explained that I was still uncomfortable and still working at being healthy. To my surprise, he disclosed that he had some troubles, too. He was once into drugs, supposedly peer pressure from his then girlfriend. This was years ago and he regretted doing it, but said it made him feel amazing when they would get high. In a twisted way, it was comforting to know he was not perfect and understanding the roller coaster of addiction. On the other hand, I could not help but think he would be lured back into the high sooner rather than later. But, there I go

My Scarlet Letter

again, assuming and criticizing because I do not trust anyone. But I threw aside my analytical half, so that I could at least enjoy someone's company for a night. We finished dinner and I drove him to his car and, yes, discussed seeing each other again. He did call and I did make plans with him but then he cancelled. Not me! He left a message saying he couldn't explain right now, but he would call me back when he could. Suspicious? Yes. The flood of ideas and what ifs were consuming my brain. Is he alright? Did I do something wrong? No, my answer came in a phone call.

    The night we went out, he said he had been clean for three months. Yet, the night of the cancellation, truth be told, he was going into a rehab facility and that is why he could not explain. So, great, he relapsed and I panicked. I wished him luck and told him to reconnect with me when he was ready. He emailed and emailed and I replied here and there. Then one day, he wrote to me wishing me all the best, saying he cannot continue to pursue someone who is not really committed to trying to start a relationship. There it was, black and white. He was right. It was not fair of me to keep stringing him along. Since then, I have not pursued one guy for fear that I would, once again, appear uninterested.

    Therefore, it was back to focusing on recovery. I no longer look in the trash to see the scraps from what my family ate (to ensure they are not lying to me) and I do not scratch down numbers of a caloric count for my sister or mother. Yes, I did that. I would estimate what they were eating based on what I saw and my detective work and had

My Scarlet Letter

scraps of paper with lines of numbers chicken-scratched on there. Sick, yes I know. I am not denying that. I mean, I could not even sit at the Thanksgiving or Christmas dinner table. I put bits of food on my plate, sat in the living room and packaged it up in a napkin, then lied about eating. I would clean up and serve everyone so that no one else had to miss out. I had no desire to chatter about anything, because it would be like the elephant in the room. I was the zombie among the beautiful, vibrant humans.

But not anymore. I am full of life and, still, sadness. I am upset about the current state of my body. I am sad that I may never have someone lovingly hold me again. Yet, I cannot let these feelings win. I cannot let that evil voice inside laugh at me and win. That devil has been torturing me for years and I want nothing more than to prove him wrong. I want to laugh at him and say, "Ha! Didn't get me, did you?!" I want to be beautiful inside and out. It is not about a number, please know that. I just want to feel at complete ease with me body and I want to prove to other women suffering like I did, that you can come full circle. It is possible to climb back out of darkness and, most importantly, it is worth the fight. The pain will subside once you commit to do the work and get better. I want this positive message and, me as a positive image, to find their minds and hearts. I want the impossible to become possible.

"I want you to see your airbag light turn on! Life matters. You matter! When that light came on, I knew I was back on the map. I registered as a person again. I was no

My Scarlet Letter

longer "a ghost". I was a work-in-progress. I was someone who was turning her life around. Only you can do it. No one could save me. No hospital, no doctor could get inside to the core of my being. Only I could commit to living. It is an amazing feeling to know that I actually did have the power to do that. Granted, I am not done. But anything worth doing, takes time and work. I keep thinking about what a great story to add to numerous other personal victories. You write your own itinerary. You can choose the next destination or where the trip end. Or you choose to be continued."

As I am walking into the Y, a woman stops me to tell me that she took one of my classes and wanted me to know how good of an instructor I am. Apparently, she used to be a fitness instructor 20 years ago and taught quite a bit. She complimented me on actually teaching and making sure people knew what they were doing in terms of form and technique. I was so surprised because I am new and she thought I had been teaching for a while, even inquiring as to where else I taught classes. Never had I aspired to teach fitness classes nor would I have ever thought I could when I was in high school. I was not an athlete and I wish I had been because I would have had healthier routines and training to follow. But I was chubby as a child and it carried into high school. And here I am starting a new chapter of health and fitness. No one at the Y knows the whole story. A few know I was "sick" and had to rebuild my health and my strength. But they do not know the extent of it. I think they

My Scarlet Letter

would respect me even more if they knew the depth of my suffering and the height of my triumphant will to live. I want to earn everything on my own and not be a pity case. I feel that if I can achieve health, balance and comfort within my body, I will be able to go further in life. But each day I do not see results challenges my willpower. I am now overweight because my metabolism is basically nonexistent. I work out everyday and still I cannot burn fat. I see others who workout less and lose weight. Why am I such an anomaly? Why won't my body trust me now? It still holds onto everything as if still in starvation mode. This makes no sense.

Sometimes I wish I did not reintroduce food. I foolishly believed my body would get into a normal rhythm because that is what everyone told me would happen. Hell, my nutritionist said she worked with people who got beautiful bodies back. My therapist said it would equalize, too. Yet, here I am in a very unhappy place. I am a walking contradiction. Happy to be alive, I suppose, but miserable in this body as well. At least when I was underweight, I could put on layers and fill out a bit. Now, I am so embarrassed to shop and I hate the way clothes look on me. I hate touching my body and looking at myself for it only reminds me of how I have failed in my recovery. Not only did I fail by letting anorexia consume me, but now I could not even recover properly.

I am furious and it would be incredibly easy to go back to where I was before. I know exactly how to do it. But I

My Scarlet Letter

want to believe that I do not have to go there ever again. It was cold, dark and lonely in that place. But how long do I wait? I have given it a year and still, here I am. I want to be a success story! But how could I go speak to someone who is where I was. They would look at me in disgust and worry about themselves getting as fat as me. I absolutely hate these thoughts. They keep me awake and probably fester inside of this body, holding me prisoner. I felt like I am being punished twice. Can you be sent to hell more than once? I was tortured mentally and physically with anorexia and chose to claw my way out toward hope. Now, someone stomped on my hands with spiked cleats, severing my fingers and dropping me back down into despair. My fingers linger on the side as a reminder of the failed attempt to rise above the disease.

Luckily, I can snap myself out of these thoughts more than I could a year ago. Talking to myself helps, believe it or not. I also turn to certain songs for strength.
Music has the power to truly touch your soul. I listened to two female artists on my path attempt a better life. Ingrid Michaelson is a singer/songwriter that my sister introduced me to. Two of her songs made a huge impact on me. I listened to "Keep Breathing" in my car and it would reinforce that at least I am still here, still breathing. At times, I would get down and I would play her song called "Giving Up" and tears would roll down my cheek as I really felt like hope was fading. Usually, I would play this one after the night eating and medication combination made me gain more than I

My Scarlet Letter

wanted to. I felt like I was doomed to be obese from that point forward. I figured, I would tell everyone, I tried and they could see that I did. I had made progress, but I was not sure there was much more written for me. I lived longer than expected, but I wanted to give up (as terrible as that sounds). Then I would switch back to "Keep Breathing" and say over and over a line from the song: "All that I know is I'm breathing, All I can do is keep breathing, now". Sometimes it would break me out of that giving up feeling and, on darker days, I felt like a freak and could not shake it.

  Another artist, India Arie, wrote a beautiful song that fits perfectly with my experience. I am so glad I found this song to keep me on track. The words to this song are almost as if she wrote this specifically for me. Art, poetry and music are the language of the soul and we would be lost without it. Each one of us will feel moved by different words, notes, colors and images, which is why it is so important to have the diversity of expression that we do. I am proud to call myself an artist and hope that India can hear of the inspiration she gives to me each time I hit play. These lyrics resonate within and around me and continue to guide my strength to fight this disease.

My Scarlet Letter

"I Choose" by India Arie[i]

Because you never know where life is gonna take you
and you can't change where you've been.
But today, I have the opportunity to choose.

[Verse 1:]
Here am I now looking at 30 and I got so much to say.
I gotta get this off of my chest, I gotta let it go today.
I was always too concerned about what everybody would think.
But I can't live for everybody, I gotta live my life for me.(Yeah)
I pitched a fork in the road of my life and ain't nothing gonna happen unless I decide.

[Chorus:]
(And I choose) to be the best that I can be.
(I choose) to be authentic in everything I do.
My past don't dictate who I am. I choose. (Yeah)

[Verse 2:]
I done been through some painful things I thought that I would never make it through.
Filled up with shame from the top of my head to the soles of my shoes.
I put myself in so many chaotic circumstances, but by the grace of God I've been given so many second chances.
But today I decided to let it all go. I'm dropping these bags, I'm making room for my joy.

[Chorus:]
(And I choose) to be the best that I can be.
(I choose) to be authentic in everything I do.
My past don't dictate who I am. I choose.

[Bridge:]
Because you never know where life is gonna take you and
you can't change where you've been.

Jen Dubis 2010

My Scarlet Letter

But today, I have the opportunity to choose. (Hey ey)
I used to have guilt about why things happen the way they did cuz life is gone do what it do.
And everyday, I have the opportunity to choose.

[Verse 3:]
From this day forward I'm going to be exactly who I am.
I don't need to change the way that I live just to get a man.
(NO!)
I even had a talk with my mama and I told her the day I'm grown,
"from this day forward, every decision I make will be my own." And hey!

[Chorus:]
(And I choose) to be the best that I can be.
(I choose) to be courageous in everything I do.
My past don't dictate who I am. I choose.

(And I choose) to be the best that I can be.
(I choose) to be authentic in everything I do.
My past don't dictate who I am. I choose.

[Bridge:]
Because you never know where life is gonna take you and you can't change where you've been.
But today, I have the opportunity to choose. (Hey ey)
I used to have guilt about why things happen they way they did cuz life is gone do what it do.
And everyday, I have the opportunity to choose.

My Scarlet Letter

I continue to listen to this song and it gives me hope and purpose. It makes me feel as though I lost three years of my life to this disease. Her words make me look forward and make me feel invincible. I am strong, despite my past. No one can put themselves where I have been enough to understand my struggles that continue. My body may never full recover and I know that. But I will be damned if I let this disease take more from me. It is my choice to live the best I can, with my suffering only strengthening my determination. No one else will really understand what I went through and what it means to be where I am.

I feel different in a way I never have before. I am not sure what it is, exactly. I have always been sensitive, but I find myself on another level of reflection. For some reason, I feel almost misunderstood by my family, but not in an ignorant way. I have been to hell and endured a massive amount of suffering throughout my disease. I cannot expect others to understand my perspective because they never will. But this sets up a division that I am more aware of each day. Yes, I am not the gauntly stare of the grim reaper anymore, but that is only the surface. No one wants to hear the reality because it is too much to handle. But hearing the reality of my life and the lives of others is validation, in some way. I absorb others emotions without trying, but I find individuals fascinating. Everyone has a story and, no matter what it is, it has a level of interest.

My Scarlet Letter

    I actually attended an AAAI/ISMA certification course. This is an organization that trains fitness instructors and personal trainers. Just to be there was a huge leap for me. Most people at these things have been doing it for their entire lives. I am brand new and never planned on it happening. I was completely out of my comfort zone and took a plunge like no other. I have to say, though, I felt so proud of myself after completing the training. Granted, it was not the most advanced, intensive training there is, but it was a stepping-stone for me. Again, no one knows my past and I was able to blend right in with the crowd and perform to the best of my ability. I did not feel like a sore thumb. I felt empowered to get better and do more. Can you imagine if there will come a day when I look toned and feel comfortable enough with my body to go to the next level? I might actually be a decent instructor. And I will have earned the respect of other instructors and my students. I continue to have hope because it is what drives me. If I have no hope, I could easily slip back into that dark hole.
    I like teaching a fitness class because it is a new challenge. Every time I do it, I am quietly proud. The class still respects me even though I am not a thin, toned instructor. This has always been my style, stepping outside the norm. Each day holds new opportunities for me to share my strength with others, and it is all I want to do. So why not see where this new endeavor can take me? My heart quivers when I feel so full of love and support for someone and I cannot wait to share it and send it. If I am meant to receive

My Scarlet Letter

the same, I know it will happen. But, if because I have neglected myself and, in turn, caused so much pain to my family and friends, I accept that I may not get to experience such love. Perhaps my purpose is to be the source for others. But, oh, how I crave it.

My Scarlet Letter

You and I
© 2009

I deserve to be happy
And so do you.
I should not place blame
And neither should you.
I am proud to be me
And you should be proud to be you.
I am imperfect, thank God,
And, indeed, you are, too.
I am thankful for everything
And you should be, too.
I promise to remember this
If you promise, too.

My Scarlet Letter

Epilogue

Light
© 2009

Light is all around us,
Every moment of every day.
Do you see it?
Close your eyes.
Did you do it?
Be honest.
Can you still see it??
All too often
We rely on others
To tell us what we see
And when we see it.
But the challenge is
To ask ourselves
What we really see…
And we see that why?
Why not ask if there is more to it?
Light can be found
Not just with the trained eyes you use everyday.
Look beyond yourself.
Suspend all prior knowledge

My Scarlet Letter

And learn that you are a powerful source of light and love.
Without your light, we grow dim.
But with the power and strength
Of your individual glow,
We strengthen each other.
Fill your heart
With love, peace, hope, joy and compassion.

My Scarlet Letter

     Coming out of such darkness and despair, my life is plagued with many queries. By every law of biology and science, my body should have given out. I was down to about seventy-eight pounds at my worst, yet still walking around and teaching one hundred and fifty or so children everyday. Why didn't I collapse? I felt it in my chest with each breath. Think about how many breaths we take in a minute, an hour, a day and think of being so aware of every sensation in your body to the point of being afraid to move. I would go to bed in shock that I made it through the day, and wake up wondering why I woke up. What was keeping the life force in my body? I did not feel that any higher power would want to save me. After all, look what I did with the gift of life. I always had visions, in my childhood, of dying young and everyone called me morbid when I mentioned it. I did not say, however, that I wanted to die, simply that I had visions of myself not reaching a certain age. I believed this was his plan for me. Why bother trying if I was not going to make it long enough to fall in love and be happy. I would never have kids or own a home because my days, hell, my hours were numbered. I had accepted that this was my destiny and continue to wait for death.

     Yet, I stayed away from hospitals. Several tried to commit me to programs, but I felt it was pointless. Why put in the effort when I have already done so much damage to my body? I will have permanent damage, even if I survive. I would forever be known as that girl and could never get this tortured time away from people's minds. If I could not get

My Scarlet Letter

back to doing normal tasks without pain or fear, there would be no life for me. I visualized my funeral, hypothesizing who would come and who would not. My friends already distanced themselves, so would they even bother to come? No casket in the room, anyways, because I would be cremated. I watched as my family milled around to different circles, shaking their heads in disappointment.

"What a shame! How sad to see this happen when she had so much potential.... Why did she do this to herself? She really could have done something with her paintings.....What a waste!" These comments made me angry because I did not choose to do this to my body. I did not have this elaborate plan of self-destruction. Shit happens! Here I was, dead, and no one knew the truth. What is worse is that more lies were being spread. I would be remembered as another casualty to anorexia...just another girl on her quest to perfection who never reached it. I could not let this foresight become reality. I wanted everyone, and especially my family, to know that I did not want this. I did not delight in this sickness. I did not think I was thin and gorgeous and I wanted to be a fun person I once was years ago. I could not let this be my legacy, predetermined or not, I had other ideas. I was going to prove everyone wrong and teach him or her to write me off so soon.

My story will not end like this. Rather, it will continue with intent and passion once suppressed by fear. Funny, I used to let my actions be dictated by the reactions of others. Now, I let truth and love guide me every step of the way. It is

My Scarlet Letter

too easy to ignore reality and recreate our own. But I love a challenge! My quality of life will not be measured around my waist and I am hopeful that one day I can say that I am completely comfortable in my own skin. I am confident in my integrity and know that I am incredibly passionate, creative supportive and loving. For now, that would have to be enough. If I wake tomorrow without breath in my lungs, at least I will have peace in my heart knowing that, today, I lived in the best, most authentic way I can, allowing love to guide me. At my funeral, there would be no pity. Instead, people would say, "I am glad that I knew Jen while she was here... and I look forward to our paths crossing again."

My Scarlet Letter

Epitaph
© 2009

Name meaning lovely, yet she never could see
The warmest of hearts, that beat so tenderly(lovingly).
Anachronism, she felt, in each of her days
As unique a woman, in a great many ways.
Not special, just kind and a little bit shy
Lending mind, spirit and hand, no matter why.
Wanting to help and eliminate guilt
Struggling to keep those walls that she built.
When one crumbled and fell, to her surprise
She was lucky she could still open her eyes.
The lids did get heavy, and her body quite frail.
Those all around her did believe she would fail.
Fighting with every strength of her being
No one prepared for what they'd be seeing.
Inside and out, the healing began
All on her own, no help from a man.
Sadly, friends had stepped back for a while
She longed for one who could make her heart smile.
Fooled into thinking she had some who might care
Alone, she realized she was only a spare.
With so much of herself left to give to the world
Perhaps now, in this loss, we will honor this girl.

My Scarlet Letter

Naturally, I had no clue what this was going to do to me emotionally. Physically, I knew gaining weight was going to be terrible and I knew, deep down, my fear of gaining too much was going to happen. I knew my body was not going to process the food like it used to in prior years. But I listened to my nutritionist, initially, because I thought she knew more than me. I figured she knew what my body could reverse, biologically. But, nothing is ever balanced with me. Of course, my body decided to hold onto every morsel and not let go! So now I had fat accumulating and still, no muscles working properly. This is where I started to build endurance to be able to walk on the treadmill and, hopefully, try some weight machines. Up until this point, I had never tried an exercise class, but my mother wanted me to try yoga so that I could relieve some stress. The class before yoga was an intense muscle class with loud music and a loud woman teaching. For whatever reason, the next week, I went early and decided to try the muscle class because there were only a couple of people in there.

I was clueless as to just how significant that decision was to my recovery. I fell in love with the class because it made me feel strong. I felt that, each time I finished a class successfully, I was one day closer to happiness. The instructor had sarcastic humor, just like me, and liked to push people to add on weights. At first, I was scared because

My Scarlet Letter

I did not want to embarrass myself by falling down or wincing in pain. No one in the class knew I was sick because I was now overweight due to my body's lack of nutrients for years. So I blended in with the human race, and found a new challenge in this class. It was the only thing that kept me from slipping back. So many anorexic individuals relapse multiple times and less than thirty percent reach a full recovery. This class made me think that I could make something beautiful out of this hideous eyesore that I had let myself become.

    I got a reputation in this class for knowing the routines and never missing a class. I was dedicated and determined, just as I always am in any task I undertake. Was I as toned as I thought I would be? Not even close.(My body remains quite angry). Even still, after about six months, my instructor needed to take a day off and the fitness director needed a substitute after realizing how difficult the program was to learn and execute properly. So she asked me to do it. I panicked and said, yes, in a moment of weakness. Then I started to get nervous about being able to teach a class of 20 when I had no experience. I am not a certified instructor and do not pretend to be something I am not. I have the utmost respect for the hellish training she went through to get her certification. I wish I had a better body so that I could do it myself. But I look like a puffy, swollen version of a typical instructor.

    I practiced and practiced until I was sore and could not move, and then practiced some more. The day came and,

My Scarlet Letter

inside, I sought validation from my instructor that I was good enough to do this. I wanted her to call after the class to see how I did. But she had a feeling I would be fine and, I was. I was humbled when people in the class came up and complimented me and said they enjoyed the class. The fitness director offered me a class of my own during the week and that is when I started another step on my journey (as I mentioned about going to the training). She asked, "That wasn't your first time teaching, was it?" I wanted to say, "No" but I was honest and told her it was, in fact, my first class. She was impressed and I was relieved.

So I have gained the respect of other instructors and participants alike. I am not where I want to be, physically, but I like being a real sized person in front of the class. I sure as hell am not perfect and never will be, thankfully. Now that I think of it, though, I know I need to be better emotionally and mentally for my body to follow suit. Perhaps I should look into polarity treatments. Well, in any case, I press on and am glad to have gotten a nudge from my instructor. I feel a connection to her, for one reason or another. She seems to know that there is more than what meets the eye, perhaps, because she is a certified medium and psychic. I only found this out recently and am intrigued by the whole idea. It raises so many questions inside of me and gives me new rays of light and new insights.

She invited me to be a guinea pig for her class of apprenticing mediums and psychics. I, along with several others, went to the church and sat in a circuit where every

My Scarlet Letter

two minutes, the students switched and I got a new reading. I was fascinated, to say the least. I was not skeptical, rather I was trying to figure out how these individuals could read vibrations and could get the clutter out of their minds to be vessels for these spirits. I still think about it. But, after "closing up shop" or closing down the church and thanking the spirits for coming to connect, she told me to pop in on Sunday when she does the messages to conclude the weekly service. She knows of my intrigue and, I am an incredibly supportive and caring person, so I wanted to come even though I know she did not need me as a support. I sat in the car for about twenty minutes before going inside. Actually, I arrived earlier than that and walked the beach for twenty minutes before sitting in my car for just as long. I was second-guessing my decision to come. Would members not want me there? Would my instructor look confused as to why I was there or, ignore my presence and not talk to me at all? I was so torn and so curious. But I would be sad if I went in and she did not want me there, or was upset that I did come because she only invited me as an obligatory courtesy. This, again, is my over-analytical mind. In reality, she probably could not care less if I came or not. She knew it would take care of itself.

    Whatever battle was going on inside, I still managed to get out of my car and walk to the door. Maybe I could just sneak in and sit quietly in the back, unnoticed. And I did just that until I saw one of the men who was in class on Friday night. As it turns out, he knows my parents and was at their

My Scarlet Letter

wedding. At first, I was thinking I made a mistake in coming as I sat with a body full of tension. My friend was not there at first, but then I saw her up front talking to all of her friends. To my surprise, she came to sit with me in the back, even though I know she prefers the front. She seemed glad that I came and introduced me to a couple of people. The church was chilly and we both commented. She said her hands were cold, but when she put them on my arm, they were warm. I said mine were colder and she said, "Yea, but they always are. But this summer they have been better." The service began with a meditation, so I was immediately tense because I know I cannot meditate correctly. I need practice and I need to learn the proper technique. She was meditating next to me and I could hear her breathing. I was so intent on trying not to seem pathetic, that I started to feel warm all over. I felt a bead of sweat forming on my temple. As the meditation ended, I could not look at her on my right, because I felt I stuck out like a sore thumb as "the one who cannot meditate".

The healing started next as the certified healers went to the sides of the sanctuary and members went to sit in the chairs in front of them. When finished, another member would come to the chair. I know I needed healing, but I knew I was not a member and did not want to jump into a seat when a member wanted a healing. Again, I wanted to remain respectful. Yet I know a healing would have done good for me. I keep thinking maybe this is the piece that has been missing. Maybe I need to nourish my spiritual soul and

My Scarlet Letter

bring peace to my internal being. I know what you are thinking. How can I quiet my mind enough to accept the positive energy? I don't know if I could. I would like to think it is possible. But I was worried that if I sat in the chair, the healer would place his/her hands on my shoulders and feel a blockage, then send me away. Or worse, they would be gathering negative ideas about me from my vibrations of anxiety. I would, no doubt, overanalyze every move of the healer. My hope is that if I do try a healing, that I will someday be able to let go and soak it up. No more soaking up everyone else's aggravations, negativities, depression and apathy. I would rise from the chair with that look of contentment I saw on everyone returning to the pews.

After this concluded, there were names read to keep in our thoughts and prayers, followed by announcements for the church. Then, they called on my instructor friend to go up and read the audience, giving messages from spirits. I did not know what to expect, but had this weird feeling inside. She left the seat beside me and immediately took over the room with energies pulling her to certain people. It was inspiring to watch her do her thing. She has been a medium and psychic for ten years so, naturally, she is very talented. Her humor entertains everyone and her confidence in what she connects with was intense. It made me anxious because I wasn't sure if she was going to have something to say to me. I do not have many "dead people" for her to speak with but I have a hell of a dark past that I was worried she would draw attention to during her talk. Then I thought, "How selfish

My Scarlet Letter

does that sound?", with fifty or so people in the room, I am sure that at least half of them have spirits dying to talk and connect with them. I believe I am spiritual, but these members have been practicing for years. I watched everyone's interactions and was jealous of the unifying bond everyone had in this sanctuary.

I felt like an outsider and didn't want them to think I was crashing their party or trying to be a follower. I just want to figure out what is going on with me. I want to know why my mind is always racing and why my body is stuck and why can't I find happiness and.....why didn't I die? Why was I kept on this earth after experiencing such hell? Is this damaged body a consequence? No one can understand this odd connection I have with death and I am simply trying to quiet my head.

Before I could keep questioning, I heard, "I'm now going to come over to Jen... Jen is way in the back. Jen took is an instructor with me at the Y. She started taking my class in Peabody and now she has her own class in Lynn. And it seems the whole Lynn Y comes here, but I dragged her here today." At this point I am frozen in my seat and tingling from head to toe. I am trying to breath deeply, but failing miserably. She told me I did not have many dead people, but she had two men with her. One was an older man, maybe a grandfather and the other a weird uncle or great uncle or something. I had to laugh because my mother's cousin was a weird, reclusive guy. She told me this out-there man cared about me a lot and had a passion for art that no one knew

My Scarlet Letter

about. His message was that I will be involved in art therapy in the future and the grandfather figure said that I would be alright financially in that job. Then she lowered the boom on me. She moved away from the spirits' messages and said how she had been meditating next to me and feeling my energy. Inside, I said, "I knew it!" but then she paused.

"I am going to tell you something you might not be ready to hear."

You could hear a pin drop and I held my breath and clenched my teeth, not knowing what would come out of her mouth. Was I doomed? Did I cheat death and now I am in some kind of limbo? Was it predestined for me to die from anorexia? Remember how I have always felt that I am going to die young. I want to live a happy life and find someone who will love me but as hard as I try, I can see everyone else around me getting married, having kids and living happily. I cannot see myself there enjoying life with anyone. Obviously, I did not know but thought she might tell me right now. She paced back and forth and glanced up in my direction, breaking the silence. She told me that I was going to be a healer! What? Me? A healer? I was completely shocked and speechless. Everyone turned to look back at me and my eyes were wide as can be. As this scene unfolded, I was truly having an out-of-body experience. It was surreal and I love surrealism. My mind and my emotions detached from my physical being sitting in that pew. She went on to say, "You will start with laying of the hands right here in this church..." And, with that said, she left me with spirit's love

My Scarlet Letter

and blessings. And I don't know what to make of all of this. Now, I overanalyze everything so, of course, I think way too much about this. It could mean nothing. It does not mean that I have to change anything about me.

But, at this point, I felt like Harry Potter. I was told I had a potential that I was clueless about and, now, had this expectation publicly spoken. How can I be great at something I don't know how to do? I would love to heal people and it feels like something I could do because I consider myself to be incredibly caring to a fault. But I had always considered myself poisonous because I was told I was always being negative. Yet, it is funny, I have felt that, since beginning my recovery on my own, I survived for a reason bigger than myself. I felt that I am here because I have a story to tell and can inspire people who may be suffering. I am here because I am supposed to be here and I am glad that I do not know what is in store for me. I figure, I have had so many visions of myself dying and not seeing myself with children or a husband that I simply cannot let these restrict and bind the spirit that is in me.

It is strange, but I feel confident in saying that I did not die because there is a bigger plan for me, I feel like I am connected with a spiritual presence because I was virtually a ghost for three years. My grandfather called me "the shadow" because he did not know when I was in the room(he still does). I was an apparition on earth, with my life breath being strangled with each passing minute. It was as if I was

My Scarlet Letter

in limbo somewhere. My body had all but expired but my mind was still quite generative, despite the immense darkness clouding over me. The poison that seeped into my brain had paralyzed my being. I was not who I truly am because this poison was controlling my every move.

So, do I really possess the power to heal? I know pretty much anyone can learn the technique of healing, but I don't want to suck at it. What do I do with that information? Do I pursue this path or am I supposed to wait and see what happens? This could be one of my missing pieces. This healing of others could, in fact, be the very thing that cements my own healing and recovery. What if I am terrible at it and do not help anyone? I do not want to fail at this. I do not want to let anyone down. I always want to help, never harm. Should I try? I think I am getting a message as I type this and am telling myself to shut up because I am getting a headache. I have my iPod shuffling songs and the Golden Smog song, "Jennifer Save Me" is playing. I think a spirit is talking to me.

Can I really save anyone? This song could be trying to tell me that I should try. How full my heart would feel if I knew that I removed a wet blanket from someone's soul. Well, that is a pretty significant action. Maybe I could help someone forget his/her worries and fill them up with positive energy and love. I have always thought I cared too much for my own good because no one ever returns the favor. My relationships are always one-sided because no one was ever thoughtful when it came to being there for me. I go above

My Scarlet Letter

and beyond, even for those that could not care less about me because I do not even register as a significant friend. I think this sign in telling me to stop focusing on that reality. It is what it is and I am not going to change who I am... and I could not if I tried. I will always care about you even if you do not do the same. So it is time to take that caring energy inside and see what happens if I use it outside of myself. That is, outside of my own head and my own family. I may be thinking too small when I should be thinking about the many, many people who need love and healing everyday. I have a feeling that I will feel the love come back in a way I had never imagined. No more will I feel as though I never receive what I give out. It is there for me to absorb and I look forward to being consumed with love. So, today and every new day following, I embark on a new journey of healing. Perhaps that is when my true happiness will reveal itself and my body will mend as mind, body and spirit finally align in harmony. Perhaps....

My Scarlet Letter

Endless Fascination
© 2007

Misanthrope?
Not really.
You fascinate me.
Each of you puts me under a spell
Speech, manner, face and spirit.
I am full of intrigue.
Idiosyncratic enjoyment,
Labyrinth of life,
Amalgamation of it all,
Filtered through your body.
Masterpieces...each and every.

My Scarlet Letter

Look Ahead
© 2009

I look ahead of me and I see possibility.
I look behind me and I see negativity.
In front of me, I reach out for warm rays of hope.
In back of me, I can still feel the end of my rope.
To my left are my failures and losses, I know.
To my right are my struggles, with which I will grow.
Above me is my limit, as high as the sky.
Below me is darkness, lying still with a sigh.
Outside me is noise, to clutter my brain.
Inside is my strength, to filter the pain.
Every angle works hand-in-hand
For sooner or later, an angel will land.

---

[i] Arie, India. "I Choose". *Testimony: Vol. 1: Life & Relationship*, Universal Republic, 2006.

My Scarlet Letter

_____

My Scarlet Letter

_____

www.ingramcontent.com/pod-product-compliance
Lightning Source LLC
Chambersburg PA
CBHW032047090426
42744CB00004B/109